Awakening '89
Notes on Culture and Politics

Heinz-Uwe Haus

Für David,
(the mentor)
Basel mit Prahw
11.05.22

Heinz-Uwe Haus

Awakening '89
Notes on Culture and Politics

edition lulu/2012

To my son, Utz-Uwe

Second edition 2012
© 2009,2012 Heinz-Uwe Haus

Cover Art: Jean Bodin
Editor: Utz-Uwe Haus
Publisher: Heinz-Uwe Haus through Lulu Inc. http://www.lulu.com/
Typeset using Adobe Garamond Pro

http://books.lulu.com/content/8117427
ISBN 978-0-557-45033-6

Contents

Contents

Foreword

The following texts, re-published as originally written, in English, for different medias and occasions, from political magazines to academic conferences in countries as different as Cyprus, Israel, Norway, Finland, Great Britain, Germany and the United States, document my views about the 1989 peaceful revolution, German re-unification and the impact of the "damages of dictatorship" in the everyday democratic practice of a pluralistic and free society.

As many others of my generation, I too experienced political involvement in self-liberation, service to my people and nation, and a once-in-a-life-time opportunity to influence policy-making in the direction I had dreamed of since my early youth.

As a historic event, the fall of the Berlin Wall marked the presumed "end" of the Cold War and the "death" of communism. In its wake the world witnessed the dissolution of the USSR; a shift in Soviet policy toward glasnost (openness) and perestroika (economic reconstruction); the revolutions of 1989 throughout Poland, Czechoslovakia, Hungary, and Bulgaria; the reunification of Germany one year later in 1990; and rapid geopolitical and global capitalist restructuring.

Ideas of freedom and democracy, which steered the Western European societies in their reconstruction after World War Two, and had inspired, since then, the hopes of the people under communist rule in Central and Eastern Europe, became in 1989 a reachable possibility for us too. From Rostock to Riga, in Silesia or at the Puszta, on the Streets of Leipzig or Sofia soon the guideline was "the return to Europe", not a "reform" or "change" behind walls and barbed wires.

After centuries of developing an inner resistance to the regime (re-confirmed by the failed open uprisings in Berlin 1953, Warsaw and Budapest in 1956, and Prague 1968) the overwhelming majority of citizens was ready for the historical opportunity of freedom, justice, democracy and social market economy, and to end, once and for ever, any totalitarian social engineering. No people or nation accepted any longer to be hold hostage by the Soviet's strategic interests.

The process was driven by the forces that were reshaping the after-war-world:

modern media and technology, mounting material aspirations and consciousness of human rights. Western radio stations, like RIAS Berlin, "a free voice of the free world", influenced millions of people and empowered them to unmask the communist propaganda and lies. Neither the Soviet occupation nor its puppet-Party-regimes could seriously undermine the all-European mindscape over the air waves. Western TV was at home wherever it could be received. Remembering Reagan's "Tear down this Wall" speech in the summer of 1987 helps explain how the post-World-War-Two division of Europe ended. Yet, it was also the result of Gorbachev's desperate struggle to modernize the Soviet Union's own unworkable system of government and pattern of alliance.

Like revolutions everywhere, this one was shaped by problems that had been accumulated for decades. As the upheaval spread and then exploded across the region, it passed a few turning points in which small groups of people, dissident leaders, reformist party politicians, Soviet onlookers and common citizens, were compelled to make historic decisions.

Those decisions largely determined that the peaceful revolution of 1989 would be dominated by the ideals of pluralistic democracy and civil rights, a region wide triumph for Western liberalism, and a "return to Europe".

Re-reading my texts as a series of spotlights on a common area, I remember the unexpected struggles we had to be understood by many of the so-called '68-establishment on the Western side. Some tried to save their own ideological agenda despite people's costs and rejected the urgency and the clear direction of joining the free Germany. Conflicts, debates and political negotiations constituted the core of the historical events 1989/90 itself. Once again too many intellectuals and artists did not live up to the demands of their professions.

I imagine that the readers, too, need to re-construct the historical context to make best use of these documents. Those who seek a straight forward integration of all available information are likely to be disappointed. There is no pretense of providing definitive answers. I do, however, perceive the collection as providing examples of reflection and information that will illuminate issues and stimulate fresh insights.

The challenges since the fall of the Wall, especially its impact on the re-shaping of a new and united Europe, are today as fundamental as twenty years ago.

As a theatre man and educator I hope that this collection encourages discussing questions such as: What are the European cultural shifts since 1989? What are the major global cultural shifts post-Cold War? How have these shifts impacted arts and humanities?

Re-reading the texts as one who tried, in a happy moment of history to be actively involved in the policy-making, I am reminded of our revolutionary goals for the creation of a European Identity in terms of culture, education, currency, trade, foreign policy, law, immigration, and borders. The interconnectedness of processes, their dialectical implications, was our guide for each next step. The Judeo-Christian civilization, with all its blessings and all its woes, offered not only a common good but also a driving force in the differing, often conflicting interpretations of the next action.

Today new challenges arise. We need, as twenty years ago, multi-faceted approaches to the problems which come with them. How far, for example, can our value system function, if we widen the space of Europe far beyond its historically grown dimensions, as some political and economic interest groups aggressively push?

This collection should prove of value to those concerned about the actuality of our main question during demonstrations and negotiations as well: How can the post-Wall-era in Europe facilitate the emergence of a new One-Europe, a free and democratic civic European community in East and West, Central, North and South, and a European Union (EU) securing the future of its people in a global world?

HUH

Stages along the way to German unity – a chronology

The peaceful revolution began in the summer of 1989. Encouraged by the perestroika policy of Soviet leader Mikhail Gorbachev, demands for change were also voiced in East Germany. Growing numbers of refugees and a lack of willingness on the part of the regime to reform created growing impatience among its citizens. Initial meetings of dissidents were held in churches and parsonages. From 4 September on demands for change were voiced publicly. The so-called "Monday Demonstrations" began in Leipzig. Peaceful demonstrations of this kind were soon being held throughout the country. On November 4 the largest demonstration in the history of East Berlin took place. The demand of the people for more participation and democracy was expressed in their chant: "We are the people!" On November 6 over 500,000 people on the streets of Leipzig were already chanting "Germany, united fatherland!".

9/10 September Neues Forum, the first countrywide political movement outside the Protestant church, was founded, calling for a dialogue about democratic reforms, with the aim, together with the largest possible participation from the population, of "reshaping" society. In the next days tens of thousands signed the proclamation "Aufbruch 89".

9 November 1989 Politbüro member Günter Schabowski mentions, apparently in passing, that the borders have been opened with immediate effect. Not long afterwards thousands of East Germans flood across the borders. After 28 years, the Berlin Wall comes down.

10 November 1989 Chancellor Helmut Kohl interrupts visit to Poland and comes to Berlin to participate in highly emotional mass rally (in front of the West

Berlin Schöneberger Rathaus) together with Hans-Dietrich Genscher (foreign secretary), Mayor Walter Momper and ailing Willy Brandt.

13 November 1989   Dresden party head Hans Modrow is tasked by the East German parliament with forming a new government. At the mass demonstrations that have been running for months there are banners reading "Germany united fatherland".

28 November 1989   Kohl presents a Ten-Point Program for "confederative structures" and a federation between the two German parts in the Bundestag for ending Germany's division.

3 December 1989   Under pressure from the party rank and file, the politburo and the central committee resign.

7 December 1989   A round table – a forum of representatives from old and new parties and organizations – convenes under the auspices of church representatives to put forward proposals to resolve the national crisis.

16 December 1989   The Advisory Council of the West German Ministry of Economics recommends uniting the two parts of Germany "under a common political roof".

19 December 1989   West German Chancellor Helmut Kohl arrives on his first official visit to the East Germany ("GDR"). In Dresden he is enthusiastically received with calls of "Helmut, Helmut" and chants of "Germany united fatherland".

20 December 1989   Modrow and Kohl agree on partnership treaty.

22 December 1989   The Berlin Brandenburg Gate is opened.

15 January 1990   Some 2,000 demonstrators storm the headquarters of the Stasi secret police in East Berlin while 100,000 demonstrate in front of the building.

28 January 1990   Representatives of the political parties agree on the formation of a transitional government. Representatives of civil rights groups are part of the round-table talks.

1 February 1990   Modrow as prime minister puts forward a draft for German unity to parliament based on military neutrality and a federal structure.

7 February 1990   The West German government decides to offer East Germany immediate talks on a currency union.

10 February 1990   Kohl and Genscher meet with Gorbachev in Moscow. Gorbachev gives fundamental assurance that the Germans may live together as one nation.

15 February 1990   Kohl reaffirms stand against German neutrality.

5 March 1990   The four largest West German publishers begin large-scale distribution of West German "press products" in the East (73 newspapers and journals).

18 March 1990   The first free elections take place in East Germany, with a conservative alliance headed by the Christian Democratic Union taking a clear victory.

12 April 1990   The first freely elected East German parliament elects Lothar de Maiziere (CDU) as prime minister.

23 April 1990   The West German government agrees on the basis of a treaty for currency union.

24 April 1990   Kohl and de Maiziere confirm in Bonn that the economic, social and currency union between West and East Germany should go into effect on July 2.

Stages along the way to German unity – a chronology

5 May 1990   First round of talks of the Two-plus-Four conferences gets underway with the six foreign ministers of the United States, the Soviet Union, the United Kingdom, France, West Germany and East Germany in Bonn. The main point of discussion is that of allegiance.

18 May 1990   Signing of a treaty for economic, currency and social union. Kohl sees this as "the birth of a free and united Germany".

1 July 1990   Currency union implemented. East Germany changes to the D-Mark. People crossing the inner-German border are no longer subject to controls.

2 July 1990   Discussions begin in East Berlin regarding the second treaty, the Unification Treaty.

16 July 1990   Kohl and Soviet leader Mikhail Gorbachev announce a breakthrough in the alliance issue. Germany is to remain a member of NATO after reunification.

22 July 1990   The East German parliament approves legislation on re-establishing the states within the country.

23 August 1990   The East German parliament approves the accession of the German Democratic Republic to the Federal Republic of Germany (West Germany) from October 3. Upon the accession under Article 23 of the Basic Law, the states of the East will become states of the Federal Republic. Berlin will be (again) Germany's capital. The Basic Law will also apply to the Eastern part of the country, with certain modifications.

31 August 1990   The unification treaty is signed in East Berlin. Both parliaments ratify the treaty on September 20 by two-thirds majorities.

12 September 1990   The Two-plus-Four Treaty is signed in Moscow. According to Article 1 of the Basic Law, united Germany will comprise the territories of the German Democratic Republic, the Federal Republic of Germany and Berlin.

The borders are confirmed as definitive. The rights and responsibilities of the four victorious powers with respect to Berlin and to Germany as a whole will end upon ratification of the treaty. Consequently, united Germany will then assume full sovereignty over its internal and external affairs.

20 September 1990   The West German Bundestag and the East German Volkskammer ratify the Unification Treaty.

24 September 1990   East Germany leaves the Warsaw Pact.

1 October 1990   Germany becomes fully sovereign. The Allies' special rights in Berlin are abolished as from 3 October.

3 October 1990   East Germany comes under the jurisdiction of the Basic Law and ceases to exist. Germany is re-united as one state. At midnight Germany's black, red and gold flag is hoisted in front of the Reichstag to the strains of the national anthem, as hundreds of thousands celebrate on the streets of Berlin and all over the country. "Day of German Unity"

It is particularly to the cultured classes that I wish to direct my remarks in the present address. I implore these classes to take the initiative in the work of reconstruction, to atone for their past deeds, and to earn the right to continue life in the future. It will appear in the course of this address that hitherto all the advance in the German nation has originated with the common people; that hitherto all the great national interests have, in the first instance, been the affair of the people, have been taken in hand and pushed forward by the body of the people.

Johann Gottlieb Fichte
1762–1814

1 Professionalism and Conformity in the GDR

Interview with Robert von Hallberg, August 27, 1990, East Berlin

One often hears intellectuals say that the present moment is depressing. Is this your experience?

I could only wish that the party intellectuals were more depressed. The fact of the matter is that many of them are now fiddling around looking for an alibi, that a lot of them are sulking, because that's the most comfortable way, they think, of coping with their past. There's a nice sentence of Brecht's: "Revolutions take place in cul-de-sacs." The thing that moves these party intellectuals is. that communism is not only at an end in reality, but also in their dreams. The crisis for many of them probably consists not so much in the elimination of the GDR, but in the fact that they took part in starting a movement that they cannot follow up without sacrificing what they call their utopia, which was, for them More than any other level of the society, the premise of life in the GDR-Stasi state. Probably everyone who lived in the GDR was more or less trained to fool themselves in everything they did. But anyone who was also professionally involved in hoping for a better world was, in the process, subject to certain temptations to suppress reality. These ladies and gentlemen-official writers, professors, and scholars-found it very easy to work for the Marxist-Leninist apparatus because it positively forces you to bottle up the inconsistency of existence in favor of pure doctrine, or to proclaim, in spirit, the rational and humane direction in which society is moving. It was among the rules of the system that the change from hardship and privileges gave these conformists an inflated sense of self-importance.

They just about managed to raise a cheer when the irksome stick had served its purpose. But they very soon missed the carrot. They've only had a problem with their identity since November 9, 1989. They stylized their own pastoral cure into an identity problem, but no one is able to share it with them. If they'd paid a hit more attention to what the people were saving, if they had staved closer to the people in their interests, they wouldn't be bitching so much now. If you look at the way people behaved at the Writers' Conference, where the only thing they discussed was their social problems, when they didn't have even one word to say for the writers who had lost their citizenship; where, on the contrary, they sent greetings and thanks for his years of leadership to Herr Kant on his sickbed ... When you think how this new PEN Club of the GDR acted in Kiel, where [Hans Joachim] Schädlich, one of those who had to leave the GDR, objected to the presence of the acting minister, Herr Höpcke, and this acting minister of culture had his name cleared by Herr Knobloch and other members' ... These people are laboring under an illusion in their dependence on and their relationship to power, where they are scarcely able to hint at their visions and utopias any more but are perplexed that things don't go on in the old way. They had gotten used to one another and had set aside moral criteria and humanistic values. The people suffered long-term harm and deprivation, but at the core they had resisted. They became more inventive than many of the intellectuals who, to this day, would rather have stuck with their 5 percent of the truth-as Stefan Heym once put it.

How is the process of self-purification proceeding now in the 'intellectual sector'?

I think it's ridiculous that the government we've elected to get rid of the GDR in short order is carrying out an intolerable policy of ensuring the maintenance of living standards in the area of scholarship and the universities. At the Humboldt University, the Marxist-Leninist section was split up into respectable-sounding institutes, so that even the most notorious Stalinists could continue teaching. The minister's answer, just before unification, was to appoint roughly an additional 150 professors from the SED cadre, under the guise of rehabilitation! Aside from a very few exceptions (Bahro, von Berg, and about five or six others), a whole mob of social scientists, Marxist-Leninists, will be changed into sociologists, or else other liberal-sounding areas of activity will be invented.2 And there will be a repetition of what is otherwise happening in reality. I think it is very important that the East German universities be thinned out, not expanded. There are enough assistants, enough freelance workers at the universities, who have both the expertise and the pedagogical and moral resources to take over the positions of existing full professors. The authorities should not be doing the reverse, leaving the old ones there and appointing additional professors from the old cadre. The continuing power of the old apparatus, and the intertwining of interests out of fear and sinecures, makes a self-renovation impossible.

In the area of culture, too, it's the case that after the elections to the Volkskammer, people from the SED party apparatus who had gotten jobs in the theater, one, two, and three years ago, were appointed to leading posts in Berlin. As late as April 15, 1990, a former member, the second secretary of the SED district administration, was promoted to manager of a theater. If you go into the GDR Ministry of Culture, you'll find the former acting minister as head of the department, because there is no head of the main department, and no acting minister any more. And at the same time he has also replaced the other acting minister who has been dismissed, so that now he functions as the head of two departments. The ministry has been reorganized so that there is an additional minister, with his personal adviser, and two secretaries of state; otherwise all that's happened -is a shift in administrative titles. Almost the whole apparatus is still there. If you go to another ministry, Health, you'll find exactly the same state of affairs. It's intolerable. For example, no jobs are advertised, not publicly, and the old party apparatus is directing things just as it did before. If you go to GDR television, where 80 percent of the people were members of the SED, you won't find that the personnel managers were dismissed, but rather that they continue to - run newly invented Offices with their same directives and "socialistic" policy. You can't expect that out of the pool of 20 percent of the people who were not party members, there will be people with enough courage and energy to fight to introduce changes. To introduce, for example, production groups which have to manage without the excessive bureaucracy of the television operation-that was originally subordinated to the security forces of the SED. Television production is no business of the Stasi. So they've got to get rid of the ladies and gentlemen of the Stasi who were in television production and not give them new jobs. That's the problem. You can go where you like and you'll see how, under the flimsy guise of expertise-"and who's to take over the new job if it isn't those who have the experience?" – the old structures are preserved. It's just a repetition of what happened in Germany after 1945.

How bad would it actually be if the situation of 1945 were now to be repeated? The old Nazis didn't rebuild the Nazi system in 1945.

The anxieties, the deformities, the harm caused by the dictator-ship-as one of our women writers put it-are so severe that people are not yet in a position to understand fully their democratic rights. In a revolutionary process like the present one, where we cannot expect that the Stalinists will resign of their own accord, the democratic forces have to gain acceptance for the rule of law in a free society, decisively, in an enlightened manner, and by the exercise of legitimate force. A number of professors, for example, must be removed from their jobs. That's a necessary step. It's not revenge, but an act designed to restore normality. We have to remove power from the hands of the people who are left and who make political decisions, among the intellectuals as well. We're not dealing with simple administrative employees. We're also not dealing with a situation in which circumstances really alter these people and force them to behave differently. To "turn around" is not necessarily a negative concept, if you understand by it the creation of objective circumstances so that people understand the need for change. But in the course of a revolutionary process of change like that, we must not forget the moral side of the matter. Up to the moment, none of the academic Stasi informants has resigned voluntarily, no one has gone of his own accord to court, no one has done anything publicly and tried to present the past in such a way as to make it possible, in the future, to create, other structures in these areas. People have merely made a 180-degree turn-at best-if they haven't, like the Mafia, managed to secure their positions on the basis of old connections, or managed to throw sand in the works. Anyone who was a paid Stasi officer or informant has to be removed by the new state. Anyone who got paid for crimes has to be removed. Anyone who, in any other way, was so corrupted by the system that he lived like a rat, must be given the opportunity, by circumstances, to develop into a civilized human being. It's not a question of revenge, not a question of persecution. It's a question of clarification, enlightenment, and justice.

We're wasting a great opportunity for intellectual and spiritual renewal. If we were to succeed at renewal in Berlin, the next few years in Europe would also be filled with substance in every respect. For instance, we could deal with the whole question of left and right in politics, of state thinking and normal thinking, the theme of federalism, the problem of security in Europe-namely, the vacuum that arises out of the disappearance of the Warsaw Pact, of a military system that was always concerned with internal oppression and gratification. A new determination of a more global responsibility would also emerge. The North-South hemispherical conflict that transcends political groups could receive stimuli from clarification of some of these issues. We should be thinking for the future and not for the past. If we don't begin this process here, the wounds in this country will become more and more severe. But the process should not be reduced to a polarity of revenge or reconciliation, because the deformities produced by dictatorship penetrated the whole society, and because victims and culprits do not stand in clear opposition to one another.

So you are not of the opinion that the intellectuals should now keep quiet.

Of course the solidarity that arose from the emergency must be kept alive by the intellectuals. But this solidarity cannot be expressed – if I can be concrete – by Heiner Müller. He was always standing on the mountains looking down into the valleys. Of course, it was pleasant and fruitful to hear from Heiner Müller that 'the GDR was only a part of a great historical process of change. There was a drop of oppositional power in this truth. But it was only an eighth or a tenth of the truth, and people fell upon this tenth of the truth. A year or even three months before the revolution, he was writing poems saying that he would cross the border and travel to Frankfurt am Main, as to a glittering and festering corpse! The many hundreds of thousands who not only had a wall, in and in their hearts, and in their city, and their hopes, shortly after they were born, never accepted this sheer historicization of the GDR. They never followed Herr Müller. No, it was the leftist smart set in West Germany and West Berlin and a few intellectuals from the GDR who were ignorant of reality. But it was, and is, nothing that could now be a vision for the concrete future. That's the way it is with their utopia. This utopia was expressed at all times, either as an exaggerated self-satisfaction, or as an object of cultural policy that had to serve the interests of the party and the Stasi.

Is the word "utopia" merely an alibi?

That cannot be emphasized too strongly. It's constantly being talked about by the so-called socialist intellectuals in the FRG. People are irritated and shocked over there. And that gives their companions the chance to keep their utopia, or to set this alibi aside. There has to be a whole new qualification of the concept, because what I have seen, for years, as left and right in this polarization, has less and less influence in concrete politics. Now for the first time utopians are being forced to name realistic notions and goals for society. In the future it's not going to be so easy to say, "The intellectuals are always on the left, art is always on the left." That's a thesis from the age of the class struggle, an invention of the twenties. It derives from blindness to, and overestimation of, the intellectuals. For the intellectuals, it is most comfortable to be as far as possible to the left, but not in relation to a party. If these people have not understood by now how for years they were exploited as useful idiots, then they should-for heaven's sake!-be taken less seriously in the future. I really think these so-called intellectuals are taking liberties in installing themselves so comfortably and then trumpeting about all over the place that the people don't understand them, that we're a people of banana-eaters and VW owners. The intellectuals all had their bananas and their VWs.

You spoke of hope, the hope of resistance? Were you not then surprised on November 9, 1989?

For the people, the only question was that there had to be an end at some point, of the Soviet occupation. Anyone here who maintains that this came as a surprise to them must never have talked to people who were farmers, or bakers, or fitters, or foresters. The path that so many intellectuals chose for themselves in their-imagination was, in reality a path trodden by people who had a special proximity to power. The GDR, provided them with a livelihood in exchange for their opportunistic compliance. Their lifelong illusion was entirely in the hands of the regime. That's why they now conjure up the myth of obstructed independence. They want to wipe out the traces of oppression, fear, and hatred, and conceal their emptiness and failure in the pale light of false thinking. For the majority of people, it was like living under an old feudal system, what I would like to call a stick-and-carrot system. It was not a state based on law, it was not a system of law. They could not sue a public or state institution. Local courts were done away with. When I was fired one day from the *Deutsches Theater* because of anti-Sovietism, because I had used texts in a production that had displeased an ideological committee of the Central Committee, I was only able to continue to have a social existence afterwards because, by mistake, someone had given written confirmation of my anti-Sovietism. They were frightened that the *Bildzeitung* would publish it. It was only later that a compromise was reached, and the notice of dismissal had to be destroyed. Someone had been so free with his rage as to write out the condemnation; otherwise you never got anything in writing. In my case, the order came from above that a compromise was to be reached. This is the sort of relationship that makes people close to the source of power-with their orders and their deformed personal relationships-continue to nurse their illusions about life.

Were you a member of the SED?

No, and I refused every time I was asked. They asked me to join three times, and three times they promised me jobs if I would join, and I didn't. That's the point: no one in this country was forced to become a member of the SED, if he wasn't interested in furthering his career, if he wasn't trying to conceal his inabilities in his chosen field, or his fears about his ability, by taking such a step. Nonparty members were unable to exploit certain functions in this country. For years they refused to give me a teaching post at the university.

That's categorical?

No, in spite of that, some people did succeed in getting a lectureship, but only a very few. But it's not necessary to have a lectureship, it's so silly. You have tote one idea better, one idea faster, and then there are gaps. Of course some people perish, careers are held up, broken-you have to be lucky. I was lucky. No intellectual can use the excuse that he had to become a member. Nobody had to do anything here. They all did it voluntarily in order to follow the path of least resistance. That wasn't necessary. There were honorable niches, and there were so many possibilities in this society to remain upright, to some limited and small degree, that this excuse doesn't wash. The people who said that they entered the party in order to improve it from inside ... all right, there may have been a few, I believe that. Not everyone who was in the party was a rogue, but there were a lot of rogues in it, and there were also upright people in it who tried, to a limited extent, to do something sensible.

How many people in your circle were not members of the SED?

In my academic circle they were all members of the SED. But in my artistic circle things were a bit easier. They were fools, at best, fools for the regime. In theater and television, and I know these well, most of them were not SED. Painters too, none of them were members.

And if they had been in the SED?

They would have received commissions and gotten their passports earlier and been able to travel. But there were also some, the majority, who weren't, and who simply ignored the illusions because of the niche they were in, and because of their work. These are the people who participated in the real intellectual development, who stayed tough, who now have a responsibility to the future. They could have become civil servants in the regime and also have been members of the party. For this reason, it's especially disgusting when intellectuals who conformed to the system present themselves today as though they had been handicapped. Of course they were handicapped, but it wasn't necessary for everyone to become a professor. They could have gotten work all over the place and given other people some hope, in the most diverse fields. Teachers play a great part in ordinary schools when they give people hope. They would never have become principals, but they could have become decent physics or biology teachers, and let it be seen by their personalities that they were concerned with the questions of youth and not with prefabricated answers. There was a place in this society for people who didn't want to accept the prescribed brainwashing. Everything else is a lame excuse in order to avoid coming to terms with the past.

First published in:

von Hallberg, Robert (editor): **Literary Intellectuals and the Dissolution of the State: Professionalism and Conformity in the GDR**. 373 p. 6 x 9, 1995, The University of Chicago Press, Chicago & London

2 Unification Implies Break with the Past

(Re)Unification was perceived to be a distant goal for future generations. In 1989 history called everybody's bluff; the Wall came down, Germans from East and West embraced and the first move towards unification had been made.

Although many non-Germans talk about reunification, most Germans now refer to current events as unification.

The apparently idle semantic quibble over (re)unification has many levels of significance. First, by insisting on 'unification' Germany implies a break with the past systems, values and attitudes which led to expansionism, militarism and war; it simultaneously lays claim to be a responsible, sovereign member of the community of European nations.

In practical terms it is hoped that 'unification' will mean the resolution of issues left over from World War II, that it will mean the end of territorial ambiguities and thus promote better international relations in Europe.

Thus, it becomes clear that unification as a description of the creation of a unitary state after decades of division refers to and involves a multiplicity of processes and attitudes both in the international community, in German national political and economic life and indeed in the psyche of the German population. Unification is more than the simple process of unifying two German states; it is relevant for us all.

Potential   For the most part Germans are aware of and sensitive to the concerns of their European neighbors. However, the very size of Germany, its geographical position, its economic might and its military potential mean that history's decision has upset the terrible stability that Europe 'enjoyed' for over 40 years.

Almost every supranational European institution will be affected.

In the European Community German unification has accelerated the drive towards integration. Some initially believed (or hoped!) that the end of the division of Europe, and of Germany in particular, would deflect attention from the economic and political integration associated with the single European Act.

9

In fact, the potential for German domination has convinced most Europeans of the need for accelerated integration. The German government has recognized this difficulty and is prepared to give up 'sovereignty' for the good of wider Europe.

Accelerated moves towards a form of European integration which will bind Germany politically and economically into a community of European nations are seen by most observers as the best guarantee against a return to 1914.

History's decision has also radically altered the German domestic political scene. For decades almost every West German paid lip-service to the cause of national unity; almost everyone deplored the lack of freedom and the economic malaise associated with the SED (former East Germany's Communist Party) regime; almost everyone expressed solidarity and sympathy with them in the East.

Now the impossible has happened, the borders are open and the citizens of West Germany are being asked to share the costs of rebuilding this part of the country.

Excessive The costs will indeed by massive. Decades of neglect and mismanagement have meant that the East German infrastructure (technical, environmental and human) has decayed so much that it is virtually incapable of adaptation; in many cases it will have to be rebuilt completely.

Unification has obviously also revolutionized party political life in Germany. Perhaps understandably, the recent elections of the freed territory identified a significant right-of-center majority in the population.

In the West, however, several states have swung away from the governing CDU to the SPD. This has been seen as a response to the excessive speed of unification under Chancellor Kohl and the economic uncertainty which it has engendered.

Perhaps the greatest losers have been the Greens; environmental issues have been perceived as peripheral to the great German debate.

Unclear While the impact of unification on national and international life is fairly obvious, it will also set in motion some less obvious processes both at home and abroad. First, the introduction of the 'social market economy' into the freed territory will involve a reorientation of attitudes.

East Germans, it is true, probably still have a collective memory of the operational principles of the market; nevertheless, it will not be easy to move from an essentially risk-free culture to one which rewards enterprise and initiative.

Also, the essential corollary of the social market economy is a functioning democracy. So far East Germans have adapted amazingly well, but new strains may yet severely test the will of those 16 million whose last experience of democracy, the Weimar Republic, was far from pleasant.

And yet, the implications of unification go deeper than even this. Once more Germans are confronted with their past. Once more they are asked to make a break with that past, and yet to remember it as they plan their future.

Just as in 1945 the former East German citizens will have to come to terms with the manner in which they lived under the SED. It is still unclear how German society will deal with those who shot others who tried to escape or those who led, worked for or simply cooperated with the Stasi, secret police.

Thus it becomes clear that unification opens up a long process, a whole series of difficult decisions and challenges, which many might have preferred to avoid.

This multi-faceted under-taking requires a positive response not only from Germans, but from us all. At last "history has decided" in the way we always said it should.

All true Europeans should rejoice. Those who harbor old resentments and prejudices should realize that it was precisely those attitudes which made 1914 and 1939 possible.

First published in:
Cyprus Weekly, Nicosia, October 5, 1990

3 United Germany – Dangers, Misgivings, Opportunities

The postwar division of Europe is gone; the burdens it imposed on Germany have been lifted. History has decided in the way we always hoped during the last 40 years. The now United Germany emerges into a different world, where in terms of self reliance and policy independence the fact of unification marks a significant change. The unification of Germany refers to and involves a multiplicity of processes and attitudes both in the international community, in German national political and economic life and indeed in the psyche of the German population.

United Germany faces an era of formidable reconstruction. It will take years of effort to repair the damage caused by division and, in the East, by four decades of communism. It will mean putting the East's rotten economy into working order and soothing worries on both sides of the fallen Iron Curtain: those of former Westerners about paying for unity's immense costs and those of former Easterners about being second-class citizens.

United Germany will face demands from their allies and neighbors that they prove themselves democratic and peace loving while fulfilling the international obligations that comes with the status of a major power. Obligations that include a continuing push for European integration and in the short run at least, a major contribution to the world security (as in the case of the multilateral buildup in the Persian Gulf right now).

In the European Community during the last months German unification has accelerated the drive towards integration. In fact, the potential for German domination has conceived most Europeans of the need for accelerated integration. The German government has recognized this difficulty and is prepared to give up "sovereignty" for the good of wider Europe. Accelerated moves towards a form of European integration which will bind the united Germany politically and economically into a Community of European nation are seen by most international observers as the best guarantee against a return to rules of the past.

But there is no doubt, that a united, powerful and more assertive Germany complicating Europe's security equation in profound but as yet unpredictable ways easily provokes suspicions and fears of different kinds. Some argue about a "disintegration" of Eastern and Central Europe before Western Europe's integration could be completed, and complain that the Berlin Wall fell too early. No comment to that. Others draw the threat that the united Germany will try to use its economic power for political purposes. They warn especially of a "neocolonialist" push by Germany into the vacuum of Eastern Europe combined with fears of German nationalism. I assume the new united Germany has to describe and to explain its position again and again and as clear as possible. But those who harbor old resentments and prejudices should realize their responsibilities in this process.

In all predicted problems, dangers and misgivings which may arise in the future fortunately no one sees a military threat or is contained by military means referring to the united Germany. This is an opportunity for the new Germany to rejoice with all other Europeans the end of the status quo.

Allow me to look into the subjects more in detail.

Let me start with the external aspects. "We want to serve peace in a united Europe and the world," proclaimed Richard von Weizsäcker as the flag unfurled in front of the old parliament building where the first German republic was proclaimed in 1918. Only a few hours earlier, the four victorious World War II powers dissolved the Kommandantura that had ruled Berlin as an occupied city since 1945, Germany reassumed full sovereignty. That simple, dignified raising of the flag was almost anticlimactic. This new Germany showed itself again in the moment of actual merger as a land where nationalism summons a great outpouring the lessons learned on a long and bitter journey through Nazism, the Holocaust, a lost war, communist terror and searing separation have been absorbed. If there is one area of real, deeply felt consensus among German political parties and voters, it is on foreign policy that is resolutely moderate and unadventurous. "With our greater weight we will not seek more power," insists Genscher, "but we will act in awareness of the added responsibility it imposes on us." No sooner had he signed the friendship treaty with the Soviet Union, for example, than he was balancing it with a call for "a transatlantic declaration between the European Community and the North American democracies." Two steps highlight the course. Genscher is charting, first, to reassure the Soviets and the world that it disclaims the use of force. United Germany agreed to reduce the armed forces from 530 000 to

370 000 over the next four years. Second, German foreign policy sets out its hopes for the 35-nation Conference on Security and Cooperation in Europe. Genscher predicted that the CSCE would soon create new institutions, including "regular meetings of heads of state... a center for conflict prevention and a secretariat." Together they could provide the multilateral foundation "for a lasting peaceful order throughout Europe."

There is no doubt, that the future of the United Germany and that of Europe are bound together. The continent divided for four decades is searching for new patterns and structures of cooperation. These positive trends are having repercussions beyond Europe. Democracy, the search for peaceful solutions and respect for human values are gaining ground in other parts of the world as well. But the successfully proven organizations and structures of the former Western alliance remain vitally important as instruments both for ensuring the security of its members and the stability of Europe as keystones of our efforts to build a new, free and democratic European order of peace. It was Dean Acheson who titled his autobiography *Present at the Creation* He was referring to the effort to rebuild the institutions of Europe after World War II. Today, we are present at the "re-creation" of Europe, if you will. We have the opportunity to shape the world for generations to come. We must not waste it.

Integration of the five new states into the Federal Republic automatically introduces a special set of relationships with Eastern neighbors. The cultural and economic links brought by the former communist administration require united Germany to develop a policy for Central and Eastern Europe, which refers to the circumstances of the last 40 years of joint socio-economic history. That need is being accelerated by apprehension about diverse, interrelated problems. Clearly, NATO must maintain itself as all irreplaceable association of Free states, joining together against aggression and prevent war.

But now the alliance can look beyond the narrower task of preventing war to the broader one of building peace. The mandate for this can be found plainly stated in Article II of the North Atlantic Treaty: "The Parties will contribute towards the further development of peaceful and friendly relations by strengthening their free institutions, by bringing about a better understanding of the principles upon which these institutions are founded, and by promoting conditions of stability and well-being."

Moving in this direction requires that we all adapt to new realities and build

upon proven collective defense structure a broader notion of security. As I understand the German foreign policy, it encourages their allies "to reassure the Central
and Eastern Europeans and the Soviets that they will not be left out of the new
Europe." But more solid dialogue and regular consultations, both military and
political are needed. There may be a virtue of having NATO reach out to all of
Europe, including neutral and non-aligned nations. The bloc-to-bloc-order of the
past 40 years is over once and for all.

The liberating democratic upheavals of 1989 adjust NATO's mission and capabilities to a world free of the conflict that divided Germany and Europe for over
a generation. It will need a lot of alignment to fight the left-wing ideology and its
argumentation in this field.

There are internal dangers and misgivings which have to do with the realization
of how much the rebuilding (Wiederaufbau) of the former East German territory
are going to cost. Too many in the old 11 states the main responsibility seems to
lie in paying bills, the new 5 states are bankrupt. You know, most of the 8 000 de-
crepit enterprises are at the verge of failure, and unemployment is heading towards
2 million, perhaps much more, out of a work force of 8.9 million. Since economic
and monetary union in July, the East's economy has been running mainly on subsidies from Bonn. Building or upgrading plant and equipment, constructing roads,
establishing communications networks and cleaning up industrial pollution are
expected to eat up more than $455 billion. This year alone, East is costing West
more than $60 billion.

Where will all that money come from? The government intends to tap private
investments, sell "unity bonds" and let the federal budget deficit grow (current
annual shortfall: $44.5 billion) a scheme that is supposed to produce $64 billion
annually for the next five years. With national elections scheduled for Dec. 2,
the government is trying to avoid talking about potential tax increases, but Kohl
concedes that "we will do what is required."

But unification's cost can not be measured in DM alone. The politico-economic
divide between East and West is paralleled by a psychological separation known as
the wall in the mind, a split that may not be overcome for a generation or more.
West German politicians and my and older generations in the East always talked as
if the two parts of Germany were essentially one. But they were separated by force
in all means: after a grinding period of intensive rebuilding, the West thrived;
while the East instability and political fragility in the region. I am very much

concerned at the shaky situation there. There is no stabilized democracy. They are in bad economic shape, and different ethnic groups are fighting again. What will we do when civil wars break out? Europe as a whole, including the united Germany, faces here uncertain developments, if it does not respond to the needs of these societies in solidarity.

For example there is that problem of unwanted immigration, since Germany has negative population growth rates and the average age is almost 47, some immigration can be absorbed. But if the economies in the Soviet Union and Central and Eastern Europe continue to decline, millions of their citizens might press westward toward the German border. It is no question that creating a stable environment will be expensive and will require big investments in Eastern Europe. But it is in the united Germany common opinion, that there is only one instrument that will help. That is the improvement of living standards there.

The legitimacy and stability of the new Europe depends on the solving of the immense problems the former communist states are in. Since the fall of the Wall no problem where ever in Europe can be singled out or belongs to one group or nation alone. The CSCE, having from outset served to ease the burden of the division of Europe, must now become even more vital as an instrument for developing structures for economic cooperation within a united continent. The united Germany looks forward to an early outcome to the CFE negotiations which are taking place in the CBCE framework and to continued progress in the talks on confidence and security-building measures, which, along with results of CSCE inter-sessional activities, will lay the necessary basis for the next CSCE summit. That summit will have to help consolidate the changes that have taken place in the former. Communist Europe, and provide substantial new impetus to, the CSCE process in all main areas of the Helsinki Final Act. To his end, implementation in letter and spirit of all CSCE obligations by all CSCE participating states remain essential. Meanwhile, I believe, the Western European and North American politicians have to speed up to determine the modalities of institutionalization without depriving the process of its flexibility and balance. CSCE's three baskets make it uniquely suited for building consensus to meet Europe's major challenges: insuring political legitimacy, economic liberty and prosperity, and strategic stability and predictability. As Secretary of State Baker stressed June 6, in Copenhagen, CSCE should "stand-upon the building blocks of democracy: Free and fair elections, political pluralism, and the rule of law." But we should not try, to make it something it is not: an alliance that can maintain the peace. Illusions in that direction as some left-wingers have, are more than dangerous.

I believe that role ultimately must continue to reside primarily with NATO. We all know what NATO has been: the most successful alliance of free nations in history and we all know what the alliance remains: bedrock of stability in the area of uncertainty, even confusion. The fact that one cannot cleanly and crisply allocate responsibilities among NATO, the EC, CSCE, and other organizations seems for some a danger. I prefer to understand it as challenge, as a chance. The unification process in Europe faces many overlapping problems, not a single one. And in my view, overlapping, multiple institutions are the commonsensical answer to those *"over there"* in the Western perception – lived under 57 years of uninterrupted totalitarian dictatorship, first under the Nazis, then under the Communists. "The people see that their future is not a prescribed time, but a free time," says Lothar de Maiziere. "This is something people did not learn, and they are afraid."

The unification purged the East of its unwished recent history, its economic and legal systems. But no amount of social engineering will be able to reach into the psyches of all East Germans and free them, virtually overnight, from their destructions. Until last year, the so-called German Democratic Republic was one of the most repressive regimes in communist Europe. Unlike Poland or Hungary or Czechoslovakia, it had no great intellectual opposition and few student rebels. Most of its known thinkers and artists were compromised by collaboration with the regime, which dispensed reward and punishment. They played no role in bursting through the Wall; in fact, many resented the very idea of unity with a multi-party, free-market society and some still do. "Where were the GDR writers and intellectual with the moral strength to fight Stalinism is well-as fascism," demands Jürgen Fuchs, a writer who was imprisoned for nine months in 1976, for "antistate activities", then expelled to the West. All power emanated from the party in a nationwide network of command and control run by the 85 000 professional operatives of the state security service, or Stasi. Ultimately it involved millions, some part-time informers, some volunteer watchdogs on party block committees in every town and village. Many of them are still working, even in important positions, in the post-communist state. I believe they revitalize their network all over the united Germany. This should be the main concern of all democrats.

The Stasi files contain the names of 6 million people, reporting on their financial problems, sexual peccadilloes and other damaging details. "Any public airing of these files, says Peter-Michael Distel, the former interior Minister of the Maiziere government until Oct, 3, "would set off a civil war." He wants restrictions on access to the records, but thousands of Germans, East and West, would like to see their, personal files so they can sue former persecutors. This issue will continue to haunt well in the united Germany. There will be for long no internal peace, if the Government of the united Germany does not succeed to destroy the syndicate of SED and Stasi as soon as possible. Just as in 1945 we are asked to make a break with that past, and yet to remember it as we plan our future. We will have to come to terms with the manner in which we lived under the communist regime. Even in the former West, many citizens must ask themselves whether their institutional contacts with the SED regime were anything more than personal convenience and whether Western indifference did not contribute to the longevity of the dictatorship.

The cold war of perceptions has left misgivings for years: Westerners as hard-boiled exploiters, Easterners as spoiled children of a socialist experiment. "There is a deep-rooted alienation between us," says Klaus Bölling, former head of the West German mission in East Berlin. "West Germans do not like the idea of sacrificing. Like rich relatives, they expect the poor relations to behave modestly, queue up and show that their fingernails are clean." The relationship will normalize, says novelist Monika Maron, who left the East in 1988, only "when the GDR is not considered a place, but rather a time, a very bad time."

But the future's demands on the Germans do not end with their internal challenges. As I explained before, they must also respond to the expectations of Europe, the US, and the world. Mindful of the memories of the Nazi horror, the old Federal Republic has maintained a relatively low political profile, avoiding great international initiatives, acting in concert with the Western European Community. Now, while never forgetting the past many are asking the united Germany to accept its leading role in Europe. Some international forces have even suggested making it the sixth permanent member of the Security Council, veto power included. That may be more than many Germans want to deal with – at least for now. But soon we will have to live up to our responsibility. Now the timers over where we could excuse ourselves because of the divided nation and the Nazi past. In my opinion the difficulties and differences, which might occur cannot outweigh the synthesis of the nation into one whole again. What counts as much is that it is a country aware of its past and firmly rooted in Europe's present and future. "History is offering us an opportunity, a rare phase in which something can be changed for the better," President Weizsäcker told us in East and West, North and South of Germany on the first full day of unity. "To unite means to share. We will be truly united when we are ready for that. And I believe most of our people want it that way."

After the pain of division, sharing the burdens and benefits of unity should make for a happier journey ahead in Germany and elsewhere too. This multi-faceted undertaking requires a positive response not only from Germans, but from all neighbors too.

Excerpts from a lecture at Haus Rissen, Hamburg, October 26, 1990

4 For Me There is No Doubt

For me there is no doubt: The past months were the happiest time of my social and political life. The escalating struggle and success in changing the almost unchangeable made it clear that the damages and the pain have become experiences resulting in strengths and courage, in which I myself had not been able to believe anymore.

But enthusiasm also can take away your breath and cloud the view. Since the Unification has been gained, the newly found freedom often totters rather than rushes forward and presents challenges daily. Sometimes the new reality can not keep pace with expectations.

After a year of total political engagements, I am forced to realize with despair that we were not persistent enough to get rid of more burdens of the past before the re-unification.

An unreasonable tolerance shown to previous oppressors has made it easy for the Party hierarchy everywhere to remain in positions and offices.

In joyous rapture over the end of the totalitarian occupation, we believed to have reached the goal of our dreams and struggles, but reality showed that we still and again have to face the old oppressors.

How can justice reign, when the criminals of yesterday move into parliament, direct banks and companies? While they may not be a serious danger for the larger part of society, for people in "Beitrittsgebiet" (GDR) they represent an unacceptable Mafia which still demands tribute. Is this what we struggled for?

I can empathize well with the insecurity of the people in the new Federal States. Before, the fear was calculable. The fear was called Stasi, SED, "Informants", and "Searches". Fear carried boots, weapons, and was armed to the teeth. Today fear is quietly walking on crepe soles; it carries no address and has learned democratic etiquette. But fear is here, omnipresent and unpredictable. Fear of unemployment and social decline, fear of the loss of apartment or house as a result of old proprietary claims. This stifling permanent fear of the "octopus" GDR is suddenly here again and inhibits many from fully experiencing true freedom. Freedom, in the material sense is after all only a substitute.

It is my hope that the "departure" of a year ago will not shrivel into a lost utopia. I find it incomprehensible that East German students demonstrate against the dissolution of faculties and institutes in social sciences at their universities. Have they already forgotten the chicanery of the Party? Why do so many of their teachers clutch to their lectures from which they more or less participated in the party-ordered brain-washing? There is hardly anyone who voluntarily takes early retirement or seeks a more respectable occupation in the interim?

It caused me great pain to search for work and integration in such a company because I always encounter the old functionaries. But I do hear of a very few cases where people like I did again find activities which they earlier could not would not or were not allowed to perform.

In spite of this, I have resolved to return to Berlin and stay there with my family, to "make a new beginning". I write these words in the United States which has been my place of work and home for years and probably will remain so for some time. But even here many tenured colleagues in Germanistics in those circles dealing with Brecht and German post-war literature, suddenly and doggedly start pasting together a mythical "Socialism-GDR" as if their hobby had been snatched away. A conceited ivory-tower mentality becomes frighteningly apparent.

One or the other in the past regarded me as an "exotic laboratory animal" and now is quite personally chagrined that I helped make a reality out of what I always prophesied: To use the very first opportunity to unseat the regime and unveil its true character.

Many of these university professors dabbling in politics might be well advised to study the behavior of their clique during the last 40 years. It is painful that not a few of them are of German descent.

Nevertheless: My personal inclinations coincide with realistic opportunities which seem to be within grasp and the realm of reality.

Newark, DE, January 1991

5 Truth is the first step toward reconciliation

Western culture has emerged as the victor in the "Competition of the Systems", as it was formerly called. But if it is left at that, if western culture is content to play its triumphant march or trusts as the top priority the capitalistic self-cure, then it will hardly do justice to the revolutionary challenge. The future tasks are not of a restorative nature. The liberal-democratic ideas rooted in the Classics consist not only of defense against external oppression but also, at the same time, in the autonomous shaping of one's own life.

Undoubtedly it was the future existence of a common European and liberal identity – not Glasnost and Perestroika – which brought sense and shape to the revolutionary upheaval in the East. This consciousness led the new democracies out of the impasse, caused by fatal post-war development, into a no longer divided Europe in freedom and peace. An offensive preoccupation with recent history is unavoidable in this process in order to be able to perceive the value and interests of other people and to anticipate the common future. But to what extent does cultural tradition still play a role in the shaping of an individual life?

Hardly fifty years have passed since the majority of the intellectual elite of our country – scientists, artists, and the clergy – watched the Nazi crimes with incredible calm. Also during the communist terror self-denial was carried to a level of perversion - recalled in this is how the dictatorship of the party was justified in terms of a social-utopian experiment, if not as the height of human aspiration. It can be considered safe knowledge that the concern with human nature does not necessary lead to humanitarianism. "The division of human dignity for ideological reasons is a key to barbarity," summarized Ralph Giordano on the occasion of November 9, 1991 in the newspaper "Neue Zeit".

The double past of the Germans – the Nazi tyranny and the Soviet SED regime – is in one way closely connected, which demands from us a special responsibility and one which will keep us busy for quite some time. Intolerant demands for an immediate coming to terms with the past are to be judged on the basis of their motives.

It is not a question of comparing the 12 years of the Third Reich with the years 1945-49 until 1989 – the Soviet Occupational Zone/German Democratic Republic did not lead an offensive war nor commit genocide – but the parallels in their exercise of power point to problems of a common nature.

Recall the Nuremberg Trials of the Nazi officials and how and what they said in response to questions about their personal knowledge and responsibility. Do they not resemble in a fatal way the statements of the communist cadre given in our day and time in Berlin or Dresden courtrooms? Neither the similarities nor the differences of these two criminal systems allow us to minimize or justify the atrocities of GDR-style socialism.

Already Freud was of the opinion that there are traumatic crucial experiences in the collective history of people, which, because they are suppressed, are forced to reappear in a disfigured form. Like a volcano, they involve the danger of new outbreaks. The vote for absolute disclosure, however, will still not be eagerly heard.

The desire to find out, in individual cases, who the informant was, will often be viewed accusingly as revenge-seeking. But by studying files, the unbelievable corruption can be measured and the power, which still lies in the State Security (Stasi) apparatus, can be broken.

The securing of the Stasi Archives will be just the first step. Equally important is the exposing of the decision mechanisms and sources of decision of the SED state. Concerning the unofficial and official accomplices of the regime, it is important not to forget the Party, the actual octopus with its tentacles. In its being and function, it was the social destructive evil. By studying the Party one can determine how the apparatus was formed as a result of verbal directives and authorizations, and how it was set and held in motion. The "damages of the dictatorship" are to be attached to the Party, a fact which only now is becoming completely clear and which everyone can determine for himself.

Every attempt to white-wash or put the second German system of injustice into perspective is to be rejected. Hans Mayer and Ernst Block – and their many follow-up speakers – are to be contradicted when they idealize the beginnings of an "anti-fascist social model". From 8 May 1945 to 9 November 1989 people were forced, through coercion and fear, to conform to and take to task their humanistic potential. (The anti-fascism strived for in the agitation and propaganda was an especially infamous weapon against all democratic movements until the middle of the 1950s.) Also all the unclear talk about "contradictions", "progressive character of development", and "the upholding of the positive" of every age is to be resisted with the concrete history of the SED. regime before one's eyes. The problems of an East-West mental growth toward one another are in second place compared to the unresolved offender-victim-antagonism. The superficial and hectic desire to bury the hatchet, which is generally recommended, the suppression of and the anger at the support of the old regime, and the urge to occupy oneself with oneself in this time of great upheaval are the main causes for the frustrations among the new citizens of the Federal Republic of Germany. The feeling that constitutional state practice accomplishes too little justice for the victims agitates people. It is incomprehensible to many of them that the apparent offenders are able to wash their hands free of guilt en masse and that their benefice can be legalized. They do not want to accept the fact that the higher officials, the compliant judges and public prosecutors, and the unscrupulous collaborators do not have to answer to the people.

"Tribunal" or "national debate" – that is not the question if the solidarity of the citizens of the former FRG is to be mobilized. The expectations are clear: No amnesty for the SED and Stasi, no statute of limitations for crimes against humanity committed by the SED regime, the restriction of the statute of limitations until 3 October 1990 for all serious crimes related to the system of the regime, removal of guilty parties from all offices and key positions, establishment of appropriate legal grounds, lifting of all privileges and special services implemented during the SED regime, strict adherence to the relative abuse clauses in the unification treaty and memorials for the victims of the communist terror in the interest of domestic and international peace. These demands of the Association of Victims of Stalinist Persecution and Terror in Germany (VVST) to the judiciary committee of the Bundestag on 19 March 1992 in Halle affect all of us.

There are no "outsiders" – neither on the Rhine nor on the Oder. The double past begins 1933 and ends 1989. Whether in state unity or during the division of the country the historical responsibility is indivisible for a people, a fact which many citizens of the former FRG find themselves confronted and uneasy with. Many want(ed) apparently not to resign themselves to the end of a Europe on the Atlantic edge. The clarity of everyday life, as well as the vision, was lost with the unification of the nation and the continent. The new reality with the demand for a common shaping of the future provides evidence of their identity. Many people, among them politicians and managers from the former FRG, who shook hands with Honnecker and Mittag much more often and longer than protocol required and who, with large loans, extended the dictatorship of the SED, find it difficult to accept responsibility for the past. This was proven in the Bundestag discussion on the formation of an historical commission. Whoever holds public office must not only constantly think through political affairs and their conditions but must also submit himself repeatedly to a self-critical test.

"The past should not be replaced simply with hypocrisy but must be inspired by the truth. The truth is the first step toward reconciliation, which, in the realization of one's own guilt, will be followed by the readiness for atonement; only then is mercy possible." Wolfgang Stegemann, who is paralyzed from the waist and confined to a wheelchair since his release from Stasi imprisonment, wrote this on the occasion of the above-mentioned "Protest of Halle". The truth of the victim is tangible. It must become a practical criteria the liberation from dictatorship to a democratic form of life shall be achieved.

March 25, 1992

Wir sind das Volk

ökologisch sozial

Demokratischer Aufbruch –

die neue Volkspartei für die vollständige Demokratisierung

Postadresse: Marienburger Straße 12/13, Berlin 1055

6 Democratic Awakening – Propositions for new European Departures. Profile of a Civic Movement Party in East Germany

"It will have to be part of the public discussion in any society to analyze the past and to come out in favor of, or against, past events where such society wishes to make a contribution toward a lasting peace and reliable security structures. The process of political and administrative integration that is going on in Europe gave and still gives rise to the hope that communist heteronomy will be overthrown forever, marking the end of the past and preparing the ground for universal and democratic solidarity"[1]. This quotation is from one of the last statements of the former East German party *Demokratischer Aufbruch* (Democratic Awakening), which fused in October 1990 with the Christian Democratic Party. The DA, founded in June 1989 mostly by church activists, officially established as an oppositional group on 2 October 1989, formed itself as a political party 17 December 1989. In its *Leipzig Program* it supported the "right of the Germans for unity" and the establishment of a social-ecological market economy. In January 1990 the party had approximately 60,000 members. The party became a voice for unification through "accession" on the basis of the Article 23 of the Basic Law of the Federal Republic of Germany weeks before the "2 plus 4" talks and established an expert round on Europe (Arbeitsgruppe Europapolitik) in Berlin as early as in December 1989. The following is an extract from a paper named "Propositions for New European Departures" issued by this party at that time; it gives as the introductions underlines, "an idea of the envisaged 'European identity' for the German nation to be unified, and problems to be solved by the Germans together and in a self-critical way"[2]. Different from the other civic movements and democratic

---

[1] Bulletin, DA-Berlin, Arbeitsgruppe Europapolitik, Nr. 2, (1990), p. 4

[2] "Für einen neuen Europäischen Beginn – Vorschläge", in "Demokratischer Aufbruch/Allianz für Deutschland", pamphlet for the election campaign (March 17, 1990)

parties, the DA favored from the beginning German and European unification as the essential goals in its fight against the communist regime. The discussions in 1989/90 looked for an optimum system of links, not maximum integration. The "close association first, then enlargement" dilemma, which the EU maneuvered itself into since then, was not yet imagined. The urgency of the situation asked for enlargement. It seemed a tempting task for the united Germany as the future middle of the EU to create a "policy of good example" or "of trusteeship for Europe". The DA tried to facilitate domestic political backing for Chancellor Kohl's policy of European integration. Here are the seven propositions:

1. The Germans who have liberated themselves from the GDR regime have experienced 40 years of fencing off. They are suffering from the effects of virtual imprisonment; suffering from the effects of virtual imprisonment; provincialism and xenophobia are typical symptoms of this. Many find it difficult to grasp the future mission of a united Europe, its "bridging function". Young people, most of all, neither know of the value and the great meaning of other cultures nor have they ever had any cross-cultural or cosmopolitan experiences that affected and aroused their sense of tolerance. We realize a depressing incapability of openly approaching anything foreign. The complex process of German unification gives a chance to transport an entirely new and viable value system, one that opposes narrow-mindedness and cultural ignorance, to the people living on this side of the Elbe River. This system would formulate our joint European responsibility. It will be inevitable, in this respect to impact historical knowledge and facts so that questions and cultural values of other people are perceived by our people and incorporated in their lives. A positive identity that overcomes the systemic pressures resulting in a mass society and simultaneous isolation can only be gained by getting over the past and starting to build one's own future in Germany and in Europe.

2. Germany must not utilize its dominant position in an isolated manner. It should make its strength available, out of all-European power... The process of European integration requires a democratic awakening to new concepts and structures. Values deeply ingrained in European history must be checked and, if found inadequate to current needs, revised.

3. We need a European policy that combines a realistic approach to the next possible steps with political vision. The quicker the relics of what used to be the GDR are removed and the walls in the people's heads are torn down, the better conditions will become for strengthening peace, freedom, and unity in Europe. Any further debate about "autonomy" or "sell-out" with regard to the winding up of the GDR only benefits the counter-revolutionary Mafia of SED and Stasi activists and puts the political and economic consolidation of our free democratic constitutional structure at risk, "us" and "them". *Ossis* and *Wessis* are word pairs that reflect poor historical awareness.

4. It is imperative ... that we set the development of democracy and civil rights going along with the progress of our economic and social union. The individual should be able to see immediately that more common ground in Germany and in Europe means more individual freedom and social justice. Above all, the continuing utopianism and fundamentalism among the West European left should be countered using the experience gained under the so called "real-socialism".

5. It should be the objective of the agreements on European unification to form a European confederation. Each nation shall be able to preserve its cultural identity on the basis of self-determinism. This process is a prerequisite for making an independent and effective contribution not only towards preventing wars but towards creating a lasting peace.

6. The people of Western Europe who, after two devastating fratricidal world wars in the first half of the century, appear to have managed to preserve peace at last. They now tend to view cases of brutal war and mass violence as products of "stone age" mentality. But it must be remembered that war has been an integral part of European civilization until very recently. Therefore, willingness to renounce use of armed force and to manage conflict in a civilized manner cannot be taken for granted automatically but requires permanent effort.

7. World peace is no longer threatened by the post-war East-West confrontation but by the North-South conflict. Europe should, therefore, become

aware of its responsibility for a partnership with third-world countries that
is based on mutual understanding?.[3]

These positions were stated at the eve of the first free elections in the GDR setting the stage for the future: the 1991 Maastricht Treaty and the common internal
market of the then twelve EC states uniting 345 million Europeans, which was
launched at the beginning of 1993. Theses thoughts were part of the spirit, which
created a Partnership and Cooperation Agreement between the European Union
and Russia in Corfu on 24 June 1994. These attitudes made it possible that on 31
August 1994, in the presence of Federal Chancellor Kohl and the Russian President Yeltsin, Germany took leave of the last soldiers belonging to the 340,000
Russian troops and the 210,000 Russian Civilians stationed on its soil. To understand the "new thinking" we have to remember the objectives of Germany's and
Europe's "re-creation" 45 years after the fall of the National Socialist dictatorship.

The 1989/90 revolution in the GDR started with the so-called Monday demonstrations in Leipzig in the early Autumn of 1989, culminated in the first free elections 18 March 1990, which ended the communist rule, secured the accession to
the Federal Republic with a timetable for monetary, economic and social union
with effect from 1 July 1990, reconfirmed its desire for national unity through its
parliament, which voted in favor of immediate accession, and reached its goals
with the signing of the Unification treaty in Berlin on 31 August 1990. For
each political step during this period towards reunification caution was required.
Even after dismantling the wall on 9 November 1989 and being confronted with
the revolution's new direction – as expressed in the change of the slogan "We
are the People" to "We are one People" – the Soviet Leader Gorbachev warned
against any attempt to force the German issue.[4] And in the GDR itself the post-
Honnecker government under Modrow, though demanding rapid reform, tried
to maintain statehood in order to re-organize the party's forces and instruments
of power. West Germany's Chancellor Kohl, therefore, proposed 28 November
1989 a ten-point program for achieving national unity.[5] It envisaged a "contrac-
tual arrangement" based on a confederal system leading to fundamental political

---

[3] ibid.

[4] Wolfgang Kraus, Zukunft Europa, Frankfurt/Main: Fischer 1993, pp. 34ff)

[5] Benno Zanetti, ed. Der Weg zur deutschen Einheit: 9. November 1989 - 3. Oktober 1990.
Munich: Goldmann, 1991, p. 256 – 265

and economic change in the GDR. He proposed that the direct negotiations with the GDR should take place within a pan-European setting under the aegis of the European Community and the CSCE.

The DA did not only promote this idea immediately, but the Berlin section of the party described. Just two days later, the need ? "to develop in this frame as soon as possible practical steps for an accession to the Federal Republic after a wait of decades".[6]

Kohl's declaration that "regaining Germany's national unity" would continue to be the crucial political objective of this government encouraged the DA to create the slogan "Unification Now" and to influence the West German and international public opinion. Kohl, however, avoided specifying a timeframe for the negotiations so as not to spark any further comment abroad about Germany seeking superpower status.

The road to unity still seemed long to both sides, especially when Gorbachev, addressing the Communist Party Central Committee, said as late as 9 December 1989 that the Soviet Union would not leave the GDR 'in the lurch', that it was Moscow's strategic ally in the Warsaw Pact and that one still had to start from the assumption of two German states, though there was no reason whey they should not develop a relationship of peaceful cooperation. "It now looks as if Gorbachev hoped to force the intractable German government leader to accept the division of Germany and the financial support of the GDR by trying to build and anti-unification front in conjunction with the Western powers".[7]

In this situation, Chancellor Kohl's style of language and choice of words became an effective instrument of national leadership. His clear position that the people themselves should be the ones to decide on the speed and the substance of unification, helped to resist the Soviet backed counter revolutionary measures of the Modrow Government and to put the Kohl Government "under pressure from below"[8], which it needed to follow up with practical measures consolidation the changes.

---

[6] Pamphlet, DA-Berlin, 30. November 1989

[7] Gerhard Wettig, The Transformation from the Cold War to Today?s Challenges, in: Aussenpolitik, Vol. 48, No. 1

[8] Next Steps – Strategic Notes, a declaration by participants of a meeting, DA-Berlin, 20. December 1989

On 15 January 1990, 150,000 people demonstrated in Leipzig, chanting "Germany – united Fatherland". The people distrusted the Modrow administration and its acts of 'change' (Wende) at the so called 'round table', which systematically sabotaged the cooperation with the civic movement and ignored the will of the people.[9] "After Honecker was finally ousted from power in the second half of October 1989, the process of dissolution in the GDR had advanced to such an extent that t restoration of the order of state on the basis of socialist principles was out of question".[10] What could not be taken for granted from the start, however, was a process of mutually escalating inhibition and inactivity within the Communist Party and its instrument of suppression, the State Security Service ('Stasi'). "It was against this background that the last Communist government leader tried in vain, after mid-November 1989, to sustain or restore the system of rule in general and the state security service in particular. What he did achieve on a substantial scale, however, was to cover up the destruction of the Stasi files incriminating the Communist regime against the opposition of the population and to enable the transfer of considerable assets to Stasi members, which not only gave the recipients financial benefits but which also, in many instances, safeguarded positions of social power".[11]

The restless activities of the democratic forces – between them the DA – against these developments were inextricably linked with the search for an answer to the new constellation of European and world politics. "Every indecision and imponderability at this transitional phase requires whether and how an appropriate response can be found to the new needs and opportunities on what soon will be an undivided continent, finally liberated from communism too"[12], announced an manifesto of the 'Praxis Group', which was affiliated with the DA since the end of December 1989.

The process of internal destabilization increased rapidly after Modrow's attempt to save even the institution of the Stasi by restructuring it as National Security Service ('Nasi'). The "history offers the real possibility for an accession to the Federal

---

[9] Helmut Herles und Ewald Rose, eds. Vom Runden Tisch zum Parlament. Bonn: Bouvier, 1990

[10] Joachim Gauck, during a discussion at the First Wendgräben-Symposium, KAS, 23. March 1991 (documented in Archiv Haus)

[11] Hans-Hermann Hertle, Chronik des Mauerfalls, Berlin: Ch.Links, 1996, p. 159

[12] The Praxis Group, pamphlet, 29. December 1989

Republic as guaranteed for all Germans in the Basic Law"[13] stated a resolution of the DA from 5 January 1990.

But still Gorbachev held back, particularly since Poland and Hungary were escaping Moscow's grasp, Romania's Ceausescu had been overthrown in December 1989, and the GDR's departure from the Warsaw pact would inevitably upset the Cold War's balance of power. From French and British quarters too came exhortations to the Germans to "take account of the legitimate concerns of neighboring countries"[14] as they pursued national unity. Finally, the unification process could only be continued after the West German government had given an assurance that there would be no shifting of the present borders, that in the event of unification NATO's 'structures' would not be extended to the territory of the former GDR, and that Germany would reduce its armed forces to offset its strategic advantage. U.S. President Bush was in favor of German unification provided the Federal Republic remained a member of NATO.[15]

During these weeks, the DA concentrated its efforts to make obvious the contradictions in Gorbachev motives and politics toward the German question. "Up to the second half of January 1990, he held on his view that the East German state could determine its internal order itself but that it must remain an internationally independent factor".[16]

Strategically the DA in coalition with all other non-communist forces tried to concentrate on the change of the internal order counting that nothing is as dangerous for an exhausted and discredited regime as the attempt to reform it.[17] But it was still unclear in this respect which other sources of funds for the preservation of the GDR should be considered if not the Federal Republic of Germany, whose will to unify was rejected by the Kremlin. This obvious antagonistic contradiction determined Gorbachev 'hour of truth'. A paper of the DA's 'Working Group European Politics' discussed four subjects: 1. Gorbachev revoked the Brezhnev doctrine – which had openly defined the existence of the East German communist regime as a Soviet invention ("without us, there is no GDR") – by allowing a westward opening of the GDR which made its existence as separate states com-

---

[13] Flyer DA-Berlin, 5. January 1990
[14] Hans Arnold, Security Options for Europe, in: Aussenpolitik, Vol. 48, No. 1, p. 87
[15] ibid, p. 93
[16] ibid, p. 114
[17] Gerhard Wettig, p. 89

pletely untenable. 2. The fact that Gorbachev relied on, above all, two external powers in the domestic and foreign policy fields: on the USA as a partner on matters of international security and on the Federal Republic of Germany as a source of economic assistance for the internal development of the Soviet Union. 3. That Gorbachev's policy of allowing 'border states' to decide freely how to tackle their own problems meant defector that they could also choose systems other than socialism and that the Soviet Union would not intervene in internal affairs. The dual function of the GDR as a clamp of the Soviet empire and as jeopardized fragment of a nation became the focal point.[18] It shifted the 'Gorbi' enthusiasm of the summer and autumn of 1989 towards the question of how it could realistically correspond with Gorbachev's intentions. It was the clear message of the DA that only the solidarity of the American President with the Germans in the East desire for ending the division of the nation and the NATO membership of a future united Germany, a move which both Kohl and Bush viewed as an absolutely essential prerequisite for unification, could create the democratic awakening the party stood for.

History has shown that these joint forces broke Gorbachev's resistance to German unification. He accepted fundamentally the right of Germans to state unity on 30 January 1990 in his meeting with Modrow in Moscow,[19] and then, mid-July that same year, to NATO membership of a future united state. "Brezhnev's prediction that the GDR as a creature of the Soviet Union which could not survive without its permanent guarantee of existence"[20] was confirmed. Gorbachev "deserves the historical credit for having given a comparatively position direction and essentially one without the use of force, to a process of change that had become basically unavoidable, given the conditions of a system which had maintained the Communist party's claim to totalitarian rule up until the late Eighties and had suppressed all efforts towards forming an organized civil society".[21] At the eve of the restoration of German unity, I wrote on behalf of the Berlin section of the DA "the postwar division of Europe is gone, the burdens it imposed on Germany

---

[18] notes of the author for a lecture at Bennington College, titled Democratic Awakening – Opportunities and Obstacles, 5 March, 1992
[19] Policy statement of Modrow before the Volkskammer on February 20, 1990, in: Europa-Archiv, 45 (1990), p. 208 – 212
[20] Hans Arnold, p. 89
[21] Ibid, p. 101

have been lifted and history had decided the way we always hoped since the end of World War II. The now united Germany emerges into a different world, where in terms of self-reliance and policy independence the fact of unification marks a significant change. The unification of Germany refers to and involves a multiplicity of processes and attitudes both in the international community, in German national political, economic and cultural life and indeed in the psyche of the German population".[22] The text reminds the public of the "opportunity to shape the world for generations to come"[23] and ends with the following: "There is not doubt, that the future of the united Germany and that of Europe are bound together. The continent divided for four decades is searching for new patterns and structures of cooperation. These positive trends are having repercussions beyond Europe. Democracy and the search for peaceful solutions and respect for human values are gaining ground elsewhere in the world in clashes of civilizations and remain vitally important as instruments both for ensuring the stability of Europe and the security of its members as keystone of our efforts to build a new, free and democratic order of peace".[24]

One of the slogans for the March elections of 1990 reads: "National, European and global responsibilities are inseparably interwoven".[25] Nine years of experience in Germany's "European departure" confirm that national, European and global responsibilities are the basis for political stability. Another slogan of this civic movements party from one of its first leaflets defines "'Democratic Awakening' – free and fair elections, political pluralism and the rule of law".[26] These demands of the 1989/90 revolution are realized through the legitimacy and stability of the new European order. There is no question that the general initial euphoria has given way to a sober assessment of what is feasible. But as in 1989/90 the democratic forces look to the progress which has actually been made.[27]

In its last press statement, the DA's 'European Politics' Working Group wrote: "CSCE's three baskets make it uniquely suited for building consensus to meet Eu-

---

[22] Open letter of the author to the members of the DA – Berlin, August 1990
[23] Ibid.
[24] Ibid.
[25] Pamphlet, DA-Berlin, 3. March 1990
[26] Pamphlet, DA-Berlin, 28. December 1989
[27] see German Unification and its Discontents: Documents from the Peaceful Revolution, eds. Richard T. Gray and Sabine Wilke, Seattle and London: University of Washington Press, 1996

rope's major challenges; insuring political legitimacy, economic liberty and prosperity, and strategic stability and predictability".[28]

Nine years of paving the way for economic and monetary union, as well as, Europe's development into a political entity have eased the burdens of the past, but that is common ground that the "Western European and North American politicians have to speed up to determine the modalities of institutionalization without depriving the process of its flexibility and balance".[29] On the agenda are the "old DA propositions":

1. Recovery and consolidation in the new federal states cannot take place unless they are closely bound up with the process of European integration.

2. Europe cannot retain its new structure without opening itself up to reformist states in Central and Eastern Europe. Economically, as well as, politically, these states must be led step by step towards the collective European and Atlantic organizations. Without coming to terms with the second German dictatorship (the communist regime), there will be no real transformation from the Cold War to today's challenges.[30]

On this basis one also can see a steady increase in the number of people who express their satisfaction with the process of recovery in the new federal states; they presently represent over 60% of the overall population and nearly 90% of young Germans in the East between the ages of 16 and 29.

Excerpt from a paper presented at the 7th ISSEI-conference, Bergen, Norway, August, 2000

---

[28]Statement, DA-Berlin, September 1990

[29]Guy Stern at a conference of The Praxis Group at Wayne State University, Detroit, USA, 13 February 1990

[30]Propositions of the DA- Berlin, 19 December 1989

7 Identity Versus Enlightenment: Tasks Of The Intellectual Life In Germany After The 1989 Revolution

A declaration of the 'Democratic Awakening' of early April 1990 reads: "For 40 years culture and the arts were subject to a political system, which was derived from the SED's limitless claims to power and truth as well as the dictatorial enforcement of so called interests of the state security ... Democratic values, humanistic attitudes and creative achievements preserved and created in spite of and against the controlling and oppressive system, will remain in the future an undisputable part of the whole German culture."[1] From the beginning, the Fall revolution had concrete goals for an all encompassing renewal. The affected institutions should be modeled after those of the Federal Republic if possible before the formal unification. *"Clean the stable now"*[2] was one of the popular slogans during spring and summer of 1990. That has happened only in part. The overall task for the German society was and is to cope with the 'socialist legacy'. All democratic forces demand as a precondition for inner unity to lay bare the past. The aim is to combine this process with the merger of a divided Europe.

The amorphous strategies for revolution used by the opposition "whose virtue was political innocence and which dreamed of peace, inner and outer justice and the preservation of nature"[3], as Ehrhart Neubert has summarized it, immobilized the anachronistic apparatus of oppression in the Fall of '89, yet was unable to fill the vacuum of power left in December. The dynamics of unification posed unexpected challenges to the citizen's movement. For many non-communist in-

---

[1] Press Bulletin Facharbeitskreis Kultur/Landesverband Berlin des Demokratischen Aufbruchs, April 1990, p. 2; cf. Heinz-Uwe Haus, 'Unification implies break with the past', Cyprus Weekly, 5 October 1990, p. 17.

[2] Poster of the Party Deutsche Soziale Union (Berlin) for the 18 March 1990 elections.

[3] E. Neubert, Eine protestantische Revolution (Berlin, 1990), p. 69. Cf. B. Zanetti, Der Weg zur Deutschen Einheit (München: Goldmann, 1991).

telleduals the values of a so-called democratic socialism (along the lines of the 'Prague spring') were internalized. In the first critical weeks after the fall of the Wall these utopian intellectuals revealed a startling ghetto-mentality of "anxiety and alarm over alienation and reckless super-imposition of identities and interests"[4]. Instead of taking the government, the leadership, ignorant of its political strength, sat down at the 'round table' with representatives of the regime until the first free elections on 18 March 1990.

Meanwhile the SED/PDS clique converted the old structures into 'legitimacy', switched ill-gotten influence and properties into legal dependencies and claims and assured the continued existence of the party in the post-communist era.

The accommodating tendencies of the newly formed democratic movement, motivated on the surface by Christian principles, have their deeper causes in the all encompassing socio-critical reflections among their intellectuals, who wished to see a connection between the immediate and future tasks.[5] These intellectual ambitions were of limited use to the revolutionary tasks of restructuring. Their importance lay in the concept that the Germany of their dreams is truly a utopia where the conflict between intellect and power is a productive conflict directed toward placing its 'identity creating meaning' in the context of a 'society of European citizens'[6]

But what about the (very few) socialist orators of 4 November 1989 who had to leave the political rostrum by 9 November?

The social models envisioned by them were experienced by the people throughout the many years as a "grandiose animal experiment on living humans"[7] according to Wolf Biermann. From the very beginning "the people have made known that they are tired of being idolized by the necromancers. Quickly and decisively they also rejected the role of hero, 'to stand firm against the pressure of the more difficult and severe life', which Christa Wolf invoked"[8]. What do we hear from the nomenklature-intelligentsia, which laments their fading identity? How do they deal with their involvement in a system in which human beings were ruined physically, psychically and mentally? Instead of recognizing that their whole

---

[4]S. Neubert, p 137.
[5]Cf. R. Bahro, Logik der Rettung (Berlin, 1990).
[6]W. Jens, Nachdenken über Deutschland, Neue Zeit, 17 December 1990, p. 2.
[7]W. Biermann, Die Zeit, 7 December 1990, p. 12.
[8]H. Noll, Beim Whisky steigt die Liebe aus dem Dreck, Die Welt, 29 September 1990, p. 17.

existence had been based on falsehood they are concerned about their 'GDR-reputation'. They paint their collapsed realm of incompetence and meanness in the whitest of whites as if it had succumbed by accident and not as a logical consequence of its very existence. Public statements made by most of the previously 'adjusted' and the party members of the former Writer's Union for example, are now designed to obscure the behavior before autumn '89 and to acquire immaculate vestments. "The twofold conflict of totalitarian attempts to dominate, is far more deep-seated than one admits"[9], explains Hans Noll.

With increasing chutzpah, the regime-guided intelligentsia hastens to divert attention from them so their bigoted approval of the 'Stasi State' will fall into oblivion. They create a myth of the 'stab in the back', in which they shape their own biography into a 'Sunday Story'. The shallow inventory of Marxist and Leninist arguments again allow them to swallow the ugliness of reality in favor of the pure theory and so hinder the underlying rational and human evolution of society.[10] But their blindness to the crimes of the left is increasingly held against them. Ralph Giordano sums it up: "The partitioning of human dignity on ideological grounds is a key to barbarism".[11] "The police state of the GDR was a grave aberration of the human spirit, even if with labels proclaiming great humanistic ideals"[12] as Friedrich Schorlemmer points out in his 'Plea for Establishment of a Political Tribunal'.

Dependent on dogma and intellectually lazy, the nomenklatura derived their arguments from Marxism-Leninism and embraced a 'salvation' which seemed to justify any sacrifice. They 'mythologize' the motives of the party's actions, which were not eo ipso reprehensible. But "it was the attempt", Schorlemmer says, "to justify crimes, professedly committed for the benefit of humanity, that was reprehensible".[13]

If the discussion has died down after short, violent starts-one thinks of the 'Christa Wolf Debate'[14] in the summer of 1990 – this is not because the present

---

[9] Ibid.
[10] Cf. L. Elm, Nach Hitler. Nach Honecker (Berlin, 1992), pp. 48ff.
[11] R. Giordano, Neue Zeit, 9 November 1991, p. 13.
[12] F. Schorlemmer, A plea for the Establishment of a Political Tribunal, Universitas, January 1992, p. 16.
[13] Ibid.
[14] Cf. U. Greiner, Keiner ist frei von Schuld, Die Zeit, 17 July 1990, p. 24; cf. H.U. Haus, Die

discarded questions would be explained, but rather the positions have hardened into a refusal to talk. A public bailing out of the scope of the 'dictatorship damages' (as Helga Schubert put it) becomes impossible. Still, as Schubert herself secretly feared, her socialist-nostalgic colleagues could one day be again in power and the bill for her remarks would come due.[15] What determines the intellectual climate in the new Länder, is the apparent inability of the evolving democratic society to lawfully dismantle the remaining network of functionaries and officials and unofficial collaborators of the Party/Stasi regime. Kurt Reinschke's appeal from May 1990 for a radical break with the intellectual Party-coterie in the humanistic and social sciences is a case in point. He insists "that present academically successful teachers and scientists, but for a few exceptions, represent a negative selection-compared to what our nation could have brought forth through a natural selection of accomplishments in the cultural and intellectual world, especially in regard to the intellectual strength and individual character".[16] The reality shows that the 'old boy network' everywhere remains in academic positions and offices.[17] This mafia hinders the long overdue rehabilitation of the formerly persecuted and delays democratization, which is the base for developing the 'inner unity'. The debate about the surviving value of a specific 'GDR-identity', which remarkably found many champions in the West, is being kept alive. The novelist Peter Schneider is one of the few who has turned against "the blurring of the contrasts between a view held earlier and now, the unobtrusive slipping into the present".[18] Of the German Left, he demands a new direction of thought and an admission of errors of judgment.

The playwright Heiner Müller contends that 'enlightenment' is a "negative force which dissolves whatever it gets its hands on".[19] Müller applies this view to culture during the GDR regime. 'Enlightenment' in the form of 'European Integration' supposedly is a simple process of 'exterminating' culture 'as it now exists in the

---

DDR war eine Zeit und kein Ort, Neue Zeit 177, 31 July 1992, p. 12. D. von Törne, Neue Zeit, 4 December 1990, p. 12.

[15] H. Schubert, Neue Zeit, 15 May 1992, p. 11; cf. P. Teupe/U. Weber, 'Wessen Straße?', Interview mit Helga Schubert, Deutschland Archiv, 25 January 1992, pp. 48 ff.

[16] K. Reinschke, Sonst waren wir vor Wiederholungen nicht gefeit, Speech at the Wartburgtreffen, May 27/29, 1990, Frankfurter Allgemeine Zeitung, 11 September 1990, p. 46.

[17] R. Leicht, Alte Kameraden, Die Zeit, 35, 21 August 1992, p. 33.

[18] P. Schneider, Die Zeit, 27 April 1990, p. 17.

[19] H. Müller, lettre international, II, Vj., 1991, p. 7.

GDR'. It aims at homogenization by destroying a 'cultural identity'; Müller even considers the 'regional and national brawls in Yugoslavia and the Soviet Union' as a 'battle over language and cultural autonomy which the threatened conquest by enlightenment legitimizes'. He summarizes: "It is a battle for sheer survival, because anyone in the house of Europe who has no language of his own is lost". Müller's view turns the nationalistic massacres in Eastern and Southeastern Europe into (justified) resistance to the cultural 'colonization' of the West.

In a commentary from July 1991 regarding Berlin after unification the novelist Christa Wolf reacted to Western doubts concerning the existence of a 'GDR-identity' with an odd analogy: It is simply not possible to 'turn the stone' beneath which an "ant tribe ... more or less kept their body and soul together" and, while "viciously denying it also identity" as it "scatters in all direction beneath the faintly disgusted looks of the observers", making inferences concerning the tribe's "way of life".[20] Wolf concedes that this may be an 'unseemly comparison', yet she adds that it was 'forced' on her by the 'cool gaze of the voyeurs', of those Western observers who were 'sneeringly' searching for the identity of the natives.

Like Müller, Wolf suggests, the analytic gaze from outside has destroyed a culture, a naturally grown 'way of life'. Beneath the stone-which means the totalitarian GDR-one lived, admittedly 'more or less' successfully, but with one identity, in a solidly constructed community. The fact that it was this very 'tribe of ants' which voted away the stone is not accounted for in her image. The demise of the GDR appears as the result of the manipulative intervention of a cold-hearted Western rationalism incapable of empathizing with authentic living relationships.

The arguments against the 'colonization' of the East by the Western consumer society, as it was and is carried forward by Müller, Wolf, Volker Braun, Stefan Heym and other authors,[21] take up resentments of traditional German criticism of civilization. Accordingly Western civilization has always been viewed as a culture destroying community. While they called up such ever present, poisonous images in Germany, they have represented socialism in spite of all criticism as the refuge of an identity. The denunciation of the Western 'Enlightenment' is supposed to strengthen the myth that, in the shadow of the dictatorship, thrived a kind of real life in terms of cultural forms or procedures. Culture thus appears as

---

[20]C. Wolf, Du – Die Zeitschrift der Kultur, July 1991, p. 18.
[21]Cf. H-U. Haus, Umwälzungen finden in Sackgassen statt, MUT, 288, August 1991, p. 26/31.

a refuge of authentic existence which does not concern itself with the question of real social conditions. Since the Wall which shielded it from the outside world has disappeared, this refuge on the initiated community is no longer being protected from the demysticising gaze of the public. The public, Müller stated in an interview, is only concerned with 'tracking down and leveling minorities'. Therefore Müller recommends as the 'appropriate way of dealing with the public': "Radically decapitate them". Though not yet held by many, this New Leftist ethnocentrism is a rising and disturbing phenomenon.

Western culture has emerged as the victor in the 'Competition of the Systems', as it was formerly called. But if it is left at that, then it will hardly do justice to the revolutionary challenge. The future tasks are not of a restorative nature. The liberal-democratic ideas rooted in the Classics consist not only of defense against external oppression but also of the autonomous shaping of one's own life.

Undoubtedly it was the promise of a common European and liberal identity-not Glasnost and Perestroika-which brought sense and shape to the revolutionary upheaval in the East.[22] This consciousness led the new democracies out of the impasse, caused by fatal post-war development, into a no longer divided Europe with the chance and obligation for freedom and peace. An offensive occupation with recent history is unavoidable in this process in order to be able to perceive the value and interests of other people and to anticipate the common future.

There are no 'outsiders'-neither on the Rhine nor on the Oder. Hardly 50 years have passed since the majority of the intellectual elite of Germany – scientists, artists, the clergy-watched the Nazi crimes with incredible calm. Also during the communist terror self-denial was carried to a level of perversion. It can be considered safe knowledge that the concern with human nature does not necessarily lead to humanitarianism.

The double past begins in 1933 and ends in 1989. German history under the Nazi tyranny and during the Soviet SED regime in one part of the state demand a special responsibility and one which will keep the Germans busy for some, time. The parallels in the exercise of power point to problems of a common nature. The democratic forces are trying to 'enlighten' the search for identity with the acknowledgement of what really happened (as for example in the case of collaboration by the churches' representatives with the Stasi). A careful study of the

---

[22]Cf. J. F. Dunn, 'A new Germany in a New Europe', Wilton Park Papers 36, London, 1991.

past is necessary, "in order to make a recurrence of this and similar dictatorships improbable".[23]

When Germans nowadays speak of bringing the two sides of their country to economic equality they speak in terms of years, but when asked how long it will take to achieve 'inner unity' and 'reconciliation of the past' they often speak of generations. 'Many eastern Germans resent the fact that some of their former oppressors are living freely and successfully'.[24]

The problems of an East-West mental growth toward one another are in second place compared to the unresolved offender-victims antagonism. The superficial and hectic desire to bury the hatchet, which is generally recommended, the suppression of and anger at the support of the old regime, and the urge to occupy oneself with oneself in this time of great upheaval are the main causes for the frustrations among the new citizens of the Federal Republic of Germany. The feeling that constitutional state practice accomplishes too little justice for the victims agitates people. It is incomprehensible to many of them that the apparent offenders are able to wash their hands free of guilt en masse and that their benefice can be legalized. They do not want to accept the fact that the higher officials, the compliant judges and public prosecutors, and the unscrupulous collaborators do not have to answer to the people.

The desire to find out, in individual cases, which the informant was, will often be viewed accusingly as revenge-seeking. But by studying files, the unbelievable corruption can be measured and the power of the Stasi can be analyzed. The ongoing discussions underline too how equally important it is to expose the decision mechanisms and sources of decisions of the Party. In its being and function, it was socially destructive. By studying the Party one can determine how the apparatus was formed as a result of verbal directives and authorizations, and how it was set and held in motion. The 'dictatorship damages' are attached to the Party, a fact which only now is becoming completely clear.

'Tribunal' or 'national debate' – that is not the question for one who cares about the 'enlightenment'. The expectations are clear: no amnesty for the SED and Stasi, no statute of limitations for crimes against humanity committed by the

---

[23] Schorlemmer, S. 17.

[24] S. Kinzer, The Sunday Dragonian, 19 April 1992, p. A13; cf. D. Blumenwitz, Kann das, was früher Recht war, heute Unrecht sein? MUT, 297, May 1992, pp. 18ff.

SED regime, removal of guilty parties from all offices and key positions, establishment of appropriate legal grounds, lifting of all privileges and special services
implemented during the SED regime, strict adherence to the relative abuse clauses
in the unification treaty and memorials for the victims of the communist terror
in the interest of domestic and international peace.[25] These demands of the Association of Victims of Stalinist Persecution and Terror in Germany (VVST) to
the judiciary committee of the Bundestag on 19 March 1992 in Halle express the
will of the majority of the Germans, who lived under 'GDR identity'. Whether
in state unity or during the division of the country, the historical responsibility
is indivisible for a people, a fact which many citizens of the pre-'89 Federal Republic find themselves confronted and uneasy with. Many want(ed), apparently,
not to resign themselves to the end of a Europe on the Atlantic edge. The clarity
of everyday life, as well as the vision, was lost with the unification of the nation
and the continent. The new reality with the demand for a common shaping of
the future provides evidence of their identity. Many Western people, among them
politicians and managers, who shook hands with the leading functionaries much
more often and longer than protocol required and who, with large loans, extended
the dictatorship of the SED, find it difficult to accept responsibility for the past.
This was proven in the Bundestag discussion on the formation of an historical
commission. "What were the pressures to which the policy of detente was exposed? What contacts among politicians and what concessions were justifiable
or not?"[26] asks Schorlemmer. The disclosures the civic movement is looking for
"should be aimed at the general public, as the whole of society has suffered deep
and long-term psychological harm"[27]

"The past should not be replaced simply with hypocrisy but must be inspired
by the truth. The truth is the first step toward reconciliation, which, in the realization of one's own guilt, will be followed by the readiness for atonement; only
then is mercy possible",[28] states Wolfgang Stegemann. The truth of the victims is

---

[25] 25. VVST-Mitteilung, Fürstenberg, März 1992; cf. Protest von Halle, Gemeinsame Erklärung
ehemaliger politischer Haftlinge, Halle, 19 March 1992 (ed. by Help e.V.), Berlin 1992; cf.
S. Kiefer, Insider öffentlich, die Andere, 30/92, p 7, he describes the activities of former Stasi-
members to build legal 'Insider committees', which insist on 'equal collaboration'.

[26] Schorlemmer, p. 20.

[27] Ibid., S. 18.

[28] W. Stegemann, Geschichte aus der DDR, Forderungen der VVST, pamphlet, FÜrstenberg 1992,

tangible. It must become a practical criterion if the liberation from dictatorship to a democratic form of life is to be achieved. "As Germans, finally, the Germans are called upon to create a political environment in Germany, through a comprehensive reappraisal of their historical responsibility ... to foster a democratic identity, which leaves extreme right-wing and left-wing ideologists without a chance of success even during difficult times."[29] The intellectual debate in Germany since the Fall Revolution of '89 is the prerequisite for the 'merging of Europe'.

Paper presented at the 3rd ISSEI-conference, Aalborg, Denmark, 1992

First published in: *Nation or Integration, Perspectives on Europe in the 90s*, edited by Ulf Hedtoft, European Studies, No. 7, Aalborg University, 1993; re-printed in: *History of European Ideas*, Vol. 19, no 1-3, pp. 301-307, 1994

S. 4; cf. Forschungszentrum aktuell, Dresden (March 1992).

[29] C. Daase/M. Jochum, 'Partners in Leadership?' United Germany in the Eyes of the USA, German Foreign Affairs Review, 43 (March 1992) p. 245.

8 (East) German Intelligentsia before and after 1989

Wolf Lepenies describes the intellectual in general as "chronically discontented"; not songs of praise, but complaints are his business.[1] He suffers from the condition of the world – and that, according to Lepenies, with justification. This reveals the problems of many East German intellectuals five years after the Wall was brought down. Even authors unburdened by nostalgia for the clear-cut distinction between East and West, or by the moral load of having been supporters of the SED-regime discover the fundamental weariness. "Something happens all the time", Irina Liebmann writes, "but not even on television is there anything worth while, even if you are all there - nothing, worlds break down, just so – boring."[2] Only "miserable scribes and vain mimes still try to attribute some meaning to their existence", Heinz Czechowski asserts, but anybody with clear vision will recognize that "we are rushing at full speed towards nothingness"[3] "One deception follows the other" Kurt Drawert writes in his "deutscher Monolog Spiegelland" (German monologue mirrorland)[4] "Do we really wake up in the new Germany to discover that the FRG is more or less a GDR", as Eckhard Mieder considers?[5]

Comprehensible criticism of the West appears to be unable to manage without the incomprehensible mystification of the East. Should there really be no alternatives for action between distress about the world and songs of praise? Is the monotony of this kind of historic pessimism more than a mere pose? To what extent is it instrumentalized by the activists, the privileged and the profiteers of the regime which broke down on November 9th, 1989? To what ideological purpose

---

[1] Wolf Lepenies, in: Martin Mayer (editor), Intellektuellendämmerung, Munich/Wien 1993, p.27, cf. Wolfgang Bergsdorf, Literatur and Politik in Deutschland, Bonn/Berlin 1992.
[2] Irina Liebmann, quoted in: Iris Radisch, Dichter in Halbtrauer, Die Zeit, Nr. 23, 4. 6. 93, p. 3.
[3] Heinz Czechowski, Nachtspur, Gedichte and Prosa, Zürich 1993, p. 217.
[4] Kurt Drawert, quoted in: Iris Radisch, op. cit.
[5] Eckhard Mieder, ibid.

does Heiner Müller oracle about the "German disaster", "colonization" or "foreign capital domination"?[6] Why is the liberation from dictatorship something "not worth mentioning" to Volker Braun?[7] Why does Christa Wolf speak of the construction of democracy in her poetry as of a "bleak, wild chase .../ nailed to the cross of the past,/ every movement/ driving/ the nails/ into the flesh"?[8] Iris Radisch diagnoses the result of an investigation and analysis of more recent works by prominent East German writers (most of them close to the GDR-regime), as "nostalgia for the GDR as it never was". These persistent tactics appear to bear fruit.[9] Roughly 30 per cent of the former "intelligentsia" today belong to the voters in favor of the SED-successor party, which is skillfully using the option of the return to power left open to it by the unification treaty. It claims to be the representative of East German interests, and it stakes its hopes on the mentality-residues of 45 years of Communist indoctrination. "Nobody needs to renounce the GDR", writes Monika Maron, "for, strange as it may seem, it appears to serve as a remedy namely of the disease of its own making: lacking self-confidence and an identity deficit."[10] Five years after the end of the dictatorship the bulk of the intellectuals who had formerly supported the system appear to have regained firm ground, not having had much trouble in considering "the disintegration of Communism as a philosophical event". Their practical collaboration has in the meantime been annulled as a theoretical misjudgment – and forgotten. Their life history has long since been transformed into a tale of woe. It is true that Communism was blown up, among other things, by the desire for individual freedom, but more fundamentally it was brought to fall by its failure to provide for the requirement of security and intellectual support. The argumentation applies to both systems: as truth and morale became historically relative parameters, the foundation of human relations, the "confidence in life" was undermined. This point entails consequences: at one blow Western liberalism was reduced from a symbol of triumph to an endangered model, since it too admits the thriving of "popular relativism", anonymity, convenience and irresponsibility.

---

[6] Heiner Müller, in: lettre international, 2. q., 1991

[7] cf. Helmut Kiesel, Die Intellektuellen und die deutsche Einheit, in: Die politische Meinung, Nr. 36, 1991, p. 49/62

[8] Christa Wolf, in: ndl 5/92, p. 33

[9] Iris Radisch, Dichter in Halbtrauer, op. cit., p.3.

[10] Monika Maron, in: Sehnsucht nach der DDR', Die Zeit, Nr. 23, 4. 6. 1993, p.1

Today more audibly than in 1989/90, when the privileged top strata had kept under the cover of "speechlessness" in an effort to divert attention from themselves, they are once again becoming actively involved as "children of the GDR" in pointing to the shady sides of liberal societies Müller bluntly declares that he had "not really learned anything new. Everything I have always known still applies" – "at any rate" as regards real Socialism and the West.[11] The unwillingness for rational discourse is conspicuous.

The writer Helga Schubert, who did not belong to the minority of the former state-supporting nomenclature laid her finger on the sore points in an interview about the difficulties of some intellectuals in coming to terms with the recent past: "It is a matter of whether one refused to accept lies or not. Everybody had the opportunity to make their choice, at work, in daily life, at school."[12] Drawert also moves the representatives of the lie into the right light.[13] The previous advocates of the former apparatus of power are called by their names. This of necessity arises for him from the maxim to assert "moral criteria also in aesthetic discourses". The true dilemma of those who could once behave as the "indispensable representatives" of real Socialism appears in the "repression process of failed elite": "Against the background of innumerable lives with broken spines they held up their sprained little finger in evidence to show that they too had protested."[14] This had happened before in Germany. Understandable that Drawert's sympathies are with those who "can be found in the obscurity of factories and in the dark corners of history, who never had an opportunity to see the light of publicity, in which the intellectuals self-righteously mirrored themselves. (...) Namely a West European left-wing movement would have good reason today for a merciless self-critical review."[15] Their sympathy with the habitualized lie and the forms of self-deception and sophisticated brutality is increasingly moving into the limelight of discussion.[16]

---

[11] Heiner Müller, Frankfurter Rundschau, 22. 5. 1993, p.5

[12] Helga Schubert, Man konnte sich weigern zu lügen, Neue Zeit, 6.11.1993, p.14

[13] Kurt Drawert, Haus ohne Menschen. Zeitmitschriften., Frankfurt/M. 1993, p.94

[14] ibid.

[15] ibid.

[16] cf. Günter Kunert, in: Sehnsucht nach der DDR?, Die Zeit, Nr. 23, 4. 6. 1993, p.6; Wolfgang Schuller, Kein schwieriges Vaterland, in MUT, Nr. 323, July 1994, p.76/87; Heinz-Uwe Haus, Als die Regisseure Gras wachsen hörten, in: Neue Zeit, 21.4.1994, p.14

Drawert's demand for the presentation of the agents of disaster, who allowed "the East to become a completely ruined region with shattered or half-shattered lives"[17] is only too understandable in the face of "dialectics" which re-coin opportunism, complicity and informing into "class-struggle". Helmut Ulrich recapitulates that: "Those who at one time seized hold of positions of power and influence were in no way elite, neither morally, nor, in many cases, professionally".[18] The latest experiences with the Union of Writers and the unification of the Academies of Art in East and West confirm that once again historic guilt is being swept under the carpet in Germany, that a necessary and inconveniently painful reappraisal is not taking place. Innumerable files substantiate that there had been central instructions by the State Security to staff key positions in the East-Academy by the Ministry for State Security. Chaim Noll calls it a "branch of the State Security".[19] The expectation of politicians in regard to self-information by the Academy members is more than naive. It is an expression of the criminal indifference displayed in passing to the agenda after the Wall was brought down. Whether in the universities, the media or cultural institutions – everywhere the spokesmen of the past have "coped" with reunification. The History Commission decided on at the 1st Congress of the Union of Writers in Travemünde, which was to investigate the role of authors of the GDR Union of Writers as culprits and victims, failed. Culprits could hardly be expected to tell the truth, the knowledge obtained would be equal to nought, Joachim Walter states.[20] Yet it is substantiated umpteen times, how the Stasi (State Security) in its "operative procedures" planned the course of the lives of its victims down to the last detail. Zealous unofficial collaborators (IM) were used to heat up differences in family life, the occasional "development" of the "version of an intimate relationship", and also the professional career (or rather career-prevention) was most carefully arranged. "Undermining" the influence of "negatively hostile persons" this was labeled. One utterance detected in the files, such as: "Every day as I read the papers I feel as though I was certified" was enough evidence to substantiate the verdict of "hostile to the state". That "undermining" activity on the part of the Ministry of State Security was also in-

---

[17] Kurt Drawert, op. cit.
[18] Helmut Ulrich, Neue Zeit, 15. 3. 1994, p.14; cf. Dorothea v. Törne, Verordnung des Wortes in Deutschland, Neue Zeit, 1. 11. 1993, p.13.
[19] at a forum of the Autorenkreis der Bundesrepublik Deutschland in Berlin, 17. 3. 1994
[20] ibid.

tensified, according to Jürgen Fuchs, in the course of the CSCE-process. The Stasi increasingly applied subtle repressive measures, since open oppression no longer appeared to be opportune. "The misuse of psychology and psychiatry took place on a massive scale" Fuchs reports.[21]

Hansjörg Geiger names the objective of the necessary enlightenment: "We need to learn, in particular for the sake of the rising generation, from an intense investigation of a dictatorial past, how a dictatorship functions, how it is dependent on a silent majority, in order to minimize as far as possible the risk of the ascent of a renewed undemocratic regime."[22]

Even the representatives of the "suppression-culture"[23] should recall how the expatriation of Biermann had introduced a process of disillusionment within their own ranks. The GDR-potential for a counter-society was spiritualized; in as far as it was not expelled to the West. Its contradictions and endurance tests for individual identity and the experience of a reduced feeling of life were repeatedly set free in this connection. C. Wolf's novel "Kein Ort, Nirgends" (no place, anywhere) is rightly regarded as paradigm of the critically-loyal GDR literature. The supposed originality of that kind of "GDR-culture" always proves to be a negative-identity: "People endured a great deal, because there was somewhere still an inkling of sense, even if they were against it ..." Müller asserted in January 1990[24] a schizophrenic attitude in between adjustment and refusal, habituation to provision by the guardian-state, and retreat into the niche-society are flatteringly described as "solidarity-community". "The rosy words of the new culture-diagnosis are either soul, substance, originality, spontaneity, naivety or disease, appearances, pollution."[25]

It is typical of the so-called "Socialist intelligentsia" to represent their partnership with the regime as an attempt to have defended ideas of a humane Socialism against Stalinism. Müller, for example, successfully managed to place that image

---

[21]Jürgen Fuchs in a forum of the Gauck-Behörde titled "Bearbeiten-Zersetzen-Liquidieren" in Berlin, 12. 1. 1994.

[22]Hansjörg Geiger, interviewed by Michael Beeskow, Mielke selbst hat die SED und die Staatsführung nicht ausspioniert, Neue Zeit, Berlin, 24. 7. 1993, p. 27.

[23]A term coined by psychologist Hans-Joachim Maaz.

[24]E. Gillen, Bilderstreit im Sonnenstaat, in: E. Gillen/R. Haarmann (editor): Kunst in der DDR, Cologne 1990, p. 19.

[25]Iris Radisch, op. cit.

in Western feature pages prior to 1989. Richard Herzinger analyses Müller's critique of Stalinism towards the end of the Eighties and concludes, that it does not go beyond a critique of bureaucracy. "Müller does not demand the protection of the rights of the individual against arbitrary state power; he rather calls for the utilization and evaluation of the collective-forming forces... instead of individual rights for the protection of the individual against the collective, Müller claims that the state should grant the right to individual; to he allowed to sacrifice themselves for the sake of the higher. Justice of the Socialist collective."[26] Those who subject Müller's plays such as "Mauser", "Zement" or "Die Schlacht/Wolokamsker Chaussee" to closer scrutiny and relate them to Müller's fluctuation between left and right-wing radical ideas, will understand why new anti-Western arguments should be added to the transfiguration of the past. Marko Martin calls this "The old Teutonic Song: culture and community versus the universality of human rights. Jüngers mythical 'Worker' in contrast to the Western 'culture vampire' "[27] It is not by coincidence that Oswald Spengler, Carl Schmitt and Ernst Jünger should have become Müller's most favorite quotation suppliers of recent years. "The failure of Socialism can now be substantiated by the argument, that it did not accomplish the break with Western civilization radically enough... Following the decadence-theory of cultural conservatism, Müller interprets the history of capitalism as a movement of the decadence of life. The division of the world now runs between a colonialist Western civilization on the one hand, and the peoples colonized by it on the other. The image of the colonized in Muller's works is invariably that of the representative of a symbiotic community ... Parallels to the romantic nationalistic ideology are conspicuous."[28] Elements of the German cultural conservative tradition of thinking marked the discourse of writers such as Müller, Braun and Wolf even in GDR-times. In an interview in 1986 Müller considered, "that the Federal Republic had no autochthon culture", that is was "far more culturally foreign-dominated than the GDR".[29] "In the East", on the other hand, "something original" had been preserved, which in the Federal Republic "is being completely overruled and killed by the Americanization and computeriza-

---

[26] Richard Herzinger, Masken der Lebensrevolution, Vitalistische Zivilisations- und Humanismuskritik in Texten Heiner Müllers, Munich 1994, p. 189.

[27] Marko Martin, Und noch ein Bocksgesang, Neue Zeit, 14. 7. 1993, p. 14.

[28] Richard Herzinger, op. cit.

[29] Heiner Müller, quoted in: Bewußtseinslage, DA-Dialog, Berlin 2/1990, p. 2.

tion of society." The inability to keep pace with Western technologization and rationalization is re-interpreted as "chance of underdevelopment", allowing an evasion of the Western principle of "acceleration". "Socialism was an emergency brake", Müller reaffirmed in 1993[30] Wolf also constantly indulges in moralizing critique of technical and scientific "blessings of civilization" and the horror-vision of "America": a concerted action of politics, cultural and arms industries. Only for Tchernobyl she has "no real address"; her "disruptive factor" was yesterday the SDI-program, and today it is the throw-away culture. "What remains" is an injustice which is neither analyzed nor localized – much to the advantage of those responsible. The flight into a critique of civilization and technology is coupled with contempt of democracy, which had not been so openly articulated by these authors before the break-down of the SED-regime, but which had always been present in their fundamentalist claims. The position of confrontation towards "The West" is also evident in the latest texts by Braun. In his poem "Wüstensturm" (desert storm) the phrase "Bagdad mein Dresden verlischt" (Baghdad my Dresden fades out) visualizes resentment against the Western conquerors of Germany in the Second World War as the real motivating force of Braun's solidarity with Iraq. Whether in Iraq in 1991, in Germany in 1945, or in the GDR in 1989/90: in Volker Braun's phantasy the West invariably has 'extinction' in mind.[31] The mentioned positions are incompatible with those of the majority of East German intellectuals, who had preserved and mediated the humanist values of Western civilization versus Socialist totalitarianism during the years of dictatorship. "How should one now behave towards artists, who had been close to the state", Monika Zimmermann asked the sculptor Wieland Forster. His reply: "What I expect of the artists is restraint. They should let a certain period of shame pass by until it may be assessed at some distance, where artistic achievement exists, and where it does not. Yet that shame-interval is missing at all edges and ends. It should, however be expected in view of the shamelessness with which enormous privileges had been enjoyed. But of course one should never confound the artist with his work. History does not ask whether a good artist had a bad character."[32] Schubert also

---

[30] Heiner Müller, Frankfurter Rundschau, 2. 5. 1993; cf. Müller's texts "Mommsens Block" and "Seife in Bayreuth", in: Mark Lammert. Blockade, Berlin 1994

[31] Richard Herzinger, Die obskuren Inseln der kultivierten Gemeinschaft, in: Die Zeit, Nr. 23, 4. 6. 1993, p. 8.

[32] Wieland Förster, interviewed by Monika Zimmermann, Machen Sie Einheitskunst, Herr

recalls that "personal indecency is simply concealed behind words such as 'grief' and 'blindness' ". Considerate behavior is misplaced: "If I think of the humiliations which were part and parcel of daily life in the GDR, I become sensitive to all attempts at revival."[33] The civil rights defender and Saxon Minister for the Environment, Arnold Vaatz, expresses that which had only been asserted inadequately between November 9th 1989 and October 3rd, 1990: "It must be prevented that old, state-supporting loyalties should simply be continued in our time. I do not want conditions of ownership to be taken over under the protection of the Constitution, which came into being because the equality principles of the Constitution had been dealt a blow in the face. I also want punishable crimes to be avenged in deed. Failure to do so would be an invitation to side again immediately with the enemies of democracy, as soon as democracy in Germany should be under any renewed threat."[34]

To sum up, it should be retained, that the division of internal unity now as before does not run between East and West, but rather between adherents to democracy and those supporting totalitarianism, between advocates of the SED-regime and those once dominated by that regime. In the fifth year of liberation we are still confronted above all with unresolved East-East conflicts; the consequences of decades of comprehensive obstruction of the advance of civilization and economic destruction, terror, injustice and tutelage. The democrats among East German intellectuals recognize the objectives which must be pursued by society as a whole: freedom, truth and justice must be asserted in the pluralistic society against their adversaries, by way of concrete preoccupation with the past and present aims of the latter. A lasting de-legitimization of the former regime and its thinking patterns will have to stop its withdrawal from history and responsibility, which has undoubtedly made progress. The controversies among East German intellectuals today have become part and parcel of the juridical, political and intellectual conflicts in Germany as a whole, which the overwhelming majority of the inhabitants of the new Federal States consider vital as a means of uncompromising and offensive consolidation of the Western links of democracy. In the face of the "twofold" German past a right to "fundamental weariness" appears as a dubious freedom.

Förster?, Neue Zeit, 17. 3. 1994, p. 6.

[33] Helga Schubert, op. cit.

[34] Arnold Vaatz, interviewed by Mathias Schlegel, Ist das Volk undankbar, Herr Vaatz? in: Neue Zeit, 4. 11. 1993, p. 6.

The apocalyptic yearning of those wishing to hold up the wheel of history calls for resistance before it is too late.

Written in July 1994 for a discussion of the Autorenkreis der Bundesrepublik at the Literaturhaus Fasanenstrasse, Berlin; published April 1996 in: The European Legacy, MIT Press, Cambridge, MA, Vol. 1, No. 2, pg. 212 – 221

9 German identity and the 1989 Revolution

The erroneous belief, that intellectuals can serve the mechanism of power without impunity, is once again condemned by history. The moment of History came when, on November, 1989, the East German masses forced the authorities to open up the intra-German borders. Without reliance on the Salvationist doctrine of socialism and without the protection of the disciplining apparatus of suppression created to protect "socialist achievements" the dictatorship and their collaborators were unable to assert their position against the unification of the both parts of post-world-war-two Germany.

With hypocrisy the SED-nomenklatura and their West German associates create a myth of the "stab in the back", in which they shape their own biography into a "Sunday Story". The shallow inventory of Marxist and Leninist arguments again allow them to swallow the ugliness of reality in favor of the pure theory and so hinder the underlying rational and human evolution of society. The "loss of Utopia" became the central slogan to denounce the liberation from communist suppression and the choice of freedom, justice, democracy and social market society.

The superficial and hectic desire to bury the hatchet, which is generally recommended, the suppression of the anger at the support of the old regime, and the urge to occupy oneself with oneself in this time of great upheaval are the main causes for the frustrations among the new citizens of the Federal Republic of Germany six years after the revolution.

The feeling that constitutional state practice accomplishes too little justice for the victims agitates people. It is incomprehensible to many of them that the apparent offenders are able to wash their hands free of guilt en masse and that their benefice can be legalized. They do not want to accept the fact that the higher officials, the compliant judges and public prosecutors, and the unscrupulous collaborators do not have to answer to the people.

"Roughly a third of all citizens in the now enlarged Federal Republic of Germany directly experienced the depths of a Communist dictatorship and subsequently the tremendous psychological strains of a revolution. Joy about the new freedom and abilities for personal development is accompanied by the disappointment of many active revolutionaries over unattained goals and the anger of the Communist losers. The other two thirds in the new Federal Republic of Germany lack this experience. However, they are called upon to assume a dominant role in shaping the future of the first third."[1]

There are no "outsiders" – neither at the Rhine nor on the Oder. The double past begins 1933 and ends 1989. Whether in state unity or during the division of the country the historical responsibility is indivisible for a people, a fact which many citizens of the former Federal Republic find themselves confronted and uneasy with, "The indifference towards, or even rejection of, the idea of the German nation in the old Federal Republic of Germany and the often accompanying enthusiasm for a 'multicultural society' is incomprehensible in the former GDR, where the idea of the nation was synonymous with emancipation from Soviet domination and liberation from Communist oppression."[2]

Many Westerners want(ed) apparently not to resign themselves to the end of a Europe on the Atlantic edge. The clarity of everyday life, as well as the vision, was lost with the unification of the nation and the continent. The new reality with the demand for a common shaping of the future provides evidence of their identity. One major difficulty, however, was that hardly anyone could predict how the process of transformation from a previously Soviet-type centrally planned economy to a market economy would develop. After the economic, monetary and social union between the two German states came into force on July 1, 1990, it became clear that the analogy to the 1948, when the Vest zones had to overcome an administratively regulated economy, was inappropriate. In the early post-war years the Vest Germans had no-one who could assume responsibility for their wellbeing; market economy and entrepreneurial initiative had survived the 15 years since the beginning of Nazi role; everyone was willing to invest time and effort to improve the dire situation. The GDR 1990, on the other hand, the effects of socialism were discernible throughout society. This applied in particular to the personnel situation: all positions in public service and in industry and commerce

---

[1] Hannelore Horn, The Revolution in the GDR in 1989: Prototype or Special Case?, in: Aussenpolitik 1/1993, p. 63.

[2] Gerhard Vettig, Shifts Concerning the National Problems in Europe, in: Aussenpolitik 1/1993, p. 70.

were in the hands of cadres which were selected on the basis of strictly Marxist-Leninist criteria. Furthermore, the implementations of transformation measures were controlled by incompetent persons who had a "class interest" in preventing change.

That problem did not only exist in the field of industry and commerce. The question of how much influence the ubiquitous apparatchiks exerted and still exert and what happens when the "fox" is asked to keep an eye on the "geese" also arises with respect to the apparatus of state, the instruments of power of the former regime (in particular to the state security apparatus Stasi and the army cadres), and within societal forces, above all the political parties. From day one of the revolution three questions were essential: How can democratic forces of society master this problem if they are systematically excluded from the real corridors of power and do not have experts in whom they can trust? How can they shape the country's economic and political development if they have to rely on former cadres in all fields? Do they stand a chance in politico-social trench warfare in which it is virtually impossible to distinguish between turncoats who have altered their convictions, opportunists, and opponents who operate undercover?

As a way out of this dilemma the first democratic elected government in the East organized a rapid integration into the Federal Republic to safeguard the overall process, but it also created delays for the "Vergangenheitsbewältigung" (coming to terms with the past), which is still on the agenda.

Many Germans in the West too, among them politicians and managers, who shook hands with the communist leaders much more often and longer than protocol required and who, with large loans, extended the dictatorship of the communist party, find it difficult to accept responsibility for the past.

"Yet the truth of the matter is that there is hardly a crime of which this state was not guilty. It was the perfection of evil and perversion in its apparatus for spying and defamation by which, in every possible way, human beings were ruined physically, psychically and mentally."[3] When Friedrich Schorlemmer, the theologian, advocated the establishment of a political tribunal to come to grips with the problems left by the communist regime, no one of this "elite" was willing to see things as they really were.

---

[3] Friedrich Schorlemmer, A Plea for the Establishment of a Political Tribunal, in: Universitas, Vol. 34, 1/1992, p. 15.

The arguments against the "colonization" of the East by the Vest, as it was and is carried forward by some prominent artists and intellectuals, take up resentments of traditional German criticism of civilization. Accordingly Western civilization had always been viewed as a culture destroying community. While they called up such ever present, poisonous images in Germany, the nomenklatura-authors have represented socialism in spite of all criticism as the refuge of an identity, as yet unhurt by Americanization and for that reason found approval among leftist West German intellectuals.[4]

The denunciation of the Western "Enlightenment" is supposed to strengthen the myth that, in the shadow of the dictatorship, thrived a kind of real life in terms of cultural forms or procedures, which was legitimized by its mere existence. Following German tradition, culture thus appears as a refuge of authentic existence which doesn't concern itself with the question of real social conditions.

Once again parts of German intellectuals are working on "a moralistic novel that deals with generational differences, repression and arrogance".[5] The real political danger of this socialist nostalgia is that it creates ideological content to the widespread popular unease at the Europe of Maastricht. It continues to spread intolerance as a reaction to the feeling of one's own weakness and inferiority.

It is an ongoing challenge for the democratic, open-minded artists and intellectuals today to help to develop tolerant viewpoints.

But tolerance requires self-confidence, and the ability to control one's impulses and to abandon comfortable prejudices.

People both desire and fear a retardation of developments. There are calls for a breather in European unification and for the increasingly reciprocal opening-up and cooperation of European countries and people. Of Course there is no alternative to further reforms in Central and Eastern Europe, to a gradual approximation of the conditions of prosperity in Vest and East, to the continuation of European integration, and to the gradual inclusion of reforming Central and Eastern European states in the EU. This is the only way Europe can effectively safeguard its role and its interests worldwide.

Throughout Europe there is a crisis of identity – national, regional, local, per-

---

[4] Cf. Konrad Low (Ed.), Ursachen and Verlauf der deutschen Revolution 1989, Berlin 1993 and Jens Hacker, Deutsche Irrtümer. Schonfärber und Helfershelfer der SED-Vergangenheit, Hamburg 1992.

[5] Frank Schirrmacher, in: Continuity or Change, Detroit 1994, p. 5.

sonal – which the arts are uniquely qualified to address. This is a political question, but only the arts can address these issues at the level at which they arise, at the level of imagination, at the level where consciousness of being part of society is formed.

Already Freud was of the opinion that there are traumatic crucial experiences in the collective history of people, which, because they are suppressed, are forced to reappear in a disfigured form. Like a volcano, they involve the danger of new outbreaks. The vote for absolute disclosure, however, will still not be eagerly heard.

Intolerant demands for an immediate coming to terms with the past are to be judged on the basis of their motives. The campaign for closing the State Security (Stasi) files – lead by the post communists and their former collaborators[6] – is obviously the try to legalize the breaking of the unification treaty.

Concerning the unofficial and official accomplices of the regime, it is important not to forget the Party, the actual octopus with its tentacles. In its being and function, it was the social destructive evil. By studying the Party one can determine how the apparatus was formed as a result of verbal directives and authorizations, and how it was set and held in motion. The "damages of the dictatorship" to use a term of the novelist Helga Schubert, are to be attached to the Party, a fact which only now is becoming completely clear and which everyone can determine for himself.

"To what extend do the former ties, loyalties and dependencies still exist in society? It is obvious that the legacy of the past cannot be eliminated in one go. Is this a matter of a generation? To what extent and how long will the Communist nomenklatura continue to influence the development in eastern as well as western Germany through obstructionism? The long arm of the GDR state security service is known to extend well into western Germany."[7]

It is one of the dirtiest totalitarian tricks to ask for self-criticism from the defeated. This could well explain their noticeable restraint in taking complete stick after the disaster of the Communist empire, especially since the history of the Left in the 20th century has been predominantly characterized by a climate of lock stepped thinking. The plea of the historian Tony Judt, for the Left, including the western Left, to do the obvious thing and come to a complete self-evaluation,

---

[6] Cf. Michael Wolffsohn, Die Deutschland-Akte, München 1994.
[7] Hannelore Horn, a.a.o., p. 65.

remains a cry in the wilderness. Judt believes that only when the Left discovers "the sober prose of everyday democratic practice"[8], can it regain the high standards in societal and political debate which one distinguished it. But what means "regain" and "high standards in former debates", if we look for a moment into their real context. Since the Bolshevik coup there was no societal and political debate between the Left which fulfilled the ethical criteria for mankind's search for meaning. On the other hand the peaceful revolution asks for a pragmatic agenda for rescuing the energy from the rubble of a collapsed utopia.

Dahrendorf, the liberal, sees the weakening of civil responsibility and solidarity as one of the main threats to modern mass democracy. He describes the future task of European societies with three catchwords: *civil society*, *community*, and *Europe*.

The concepts "civil society" and "community" also take into account the events in Eastern Europe during the eighties. In a remarkable reversal of the direction of influence, it was from there that the concept "civil society" returned to the western European debate, particularly among the Left. The short blossoming of a spontaneous civil society, separate from the state, as found in eastern Europe during the eighties, should not only receive a positive appraisal in Dahrendorf's article, but also gives rise to a skeptical question. Without wanting to devalue the close ties of natural community – everything that eastern European intellectuals like Vaclav Havel associated with the word "home", much to the surprise of many intellectuals in western Europe – Dahrendorf stresses the ideal of the "heterogeneous" nation state which is to grow into the world society. He accuses the German Left of having "failed to understand the civilizing effect of the heterogeneous nation state".[9]

I talk about a Left, which still fights the democratic society with the liberal institutions of a constitutional state based on a free market economy. This Left is using the concept of "civil society" unacceptably as an antithesis to the concept of the liberal constitutional state. They are transforming the idea of civil society into an ersatz ideology of the Left.

"If a 'civil society' – as an essential prerequisite in the long term for the realization of Western value concepts – is to develop, only a national framework can provide the starting-point given the conditions which prevail in Eastern Europe.

---

[8] Tony Judt, in: Continuity or Change, a.a.o., p. 27.

[9] Ralf Dahrendorf, in: Continuity or Change, Kyklos Nicosia, p. 63.

Under these circumstances, calling upon East European peoples to overcome their 'national restrictedness' would merely have a counterproductive impact. As experienced by the Western part of the continent in an earlier phase in history, the countries of Eastern Europe must go through the development of nationalism before they can work towards goals which lie further afield."[10]

However, the fact that the concepts of nation and nationalism reappeared on the agenda had little to do with German idiosyncrasies as it calls for a specific German answer, irrespective of whether post-national or in the sense of a conservative revolution.

The strongest polarization is currently being caused by the concepts "nation" and "nationalism". In Germany's case, "the step from the acceptably national to the unacceptably nationalist is smaller than in many other places." The success of the Federal Republic's liberal principles has proved that the "emphasis on the national" is dispensable. It would be erroneous, in the serious financial situation after reunification, to appeal to national sentiments in order to balance the books. In my view it is essential not to forget, that the "civil society" which the West German State had become after the war had created its own loyalty and solidarity without having to return to the myth of nation and nationalism.

For Germans perhaps the greatest challenge, though, will be to avoid the political ennui that accompanies "the political exhaustion the populace may feel when it confronts its continuing frustration and disappointment at being unable to overcome the established political culture. The problems and challenges posed by reunification along with the need to bring about a national reorientation to meet the demands of post-Cold War world could overwhelm the national consciousness that the opportunity to bring about progressive political change could be forced off the agenda, resulting in a collective retreat to old, familiar patterns of political control that offer little hope of change or innovation."[11]

The conflicts between nation and Europe, between nation and Western ties, ultimately only cloak an "incapacity for active solidarity within a community, both internally and externally"[12], as Wolfgang Schäuble emphasized in this context. A concordance of this discordant has to be reckoned with, to the extent that in

---

[10] Gerhard Vettig, a.a.o., p. 71.

[11] K. Michael Prince, Germany, Europe and the Dilemma of Democratic Legitimation, in: Aussenpolitik, 1/95, p. 12

[12] Wolfgang Schäuble, in: Continuity or Change, a.a.Q., p. 45.

the long term communities based on old origins and traditions will permeate the nation as the solely effective framework for the realization of civil rights and the deepening of integration. We have to see Maastricht as the opportunity to realize this equilibrium of identities in an institutional way. The crucial question is whether the most important European nations will form a political entity that can survive against the global competition. It is only secondary by comparison – as Panayiotis Kondylis, the author of a book on "Planetary Politics after the Cold War"[13] puts it – whether this aim will be achieved through the hegemony of a single nation or by means of other institutional structures.

In future, therefore, "the Parliament, Council and Commission of the EU should not focus on institutional reforms but turn their attention to the ability to act and to democratic legitimation."[14]

"Institution-building" has come a long way. What is needed now is "policy-making". If the EU takes up the major issues of the future the Germans and the other peoples of Europe will "grow into the European mould"[15], as Martin Walser assumes.

Written 1995, paper for the 5th ISSEI-conference, 1996, at Utrecht, first published in the conference proceedings.

---

[13] Cf. Panayiotis Kondylis, Planetary Politics after the War, New York, 1990.
[14] Reinhard Stuth, Europe - Tired of Change?, in: Aussenpolitik, 1/94, p. 39.
[15] Martin Walser, Über Deutschland Reden, Frankfurt/Main, 1989, p. 132.

10 Cultural and Political Challenges: The Dialectics of European Identity

If we talk about identity, we have not to forget, why the people said "no" to communism.

1. Because of its cynical conception of human rights. Rights were granted to individuals by the state in exchange for loyal social behavior. Such an understanding and practice was meant to justify the state's cruel control of the destinies of the people in the name of revolutionary ideals. The regime "graciously" granted to people what it had first ruthlessly deprived them of.

2. The Central and Eastern European revolution was directed against the communist "command economy."

3. The revolution pulled down the central pillar in political structure of socialist society: the permanent and unconditioned monopoly of power hold by the Communist Party and its government.

The party of Marxist Leninist acted as authentic interpreter and implementer of the monolithic will of the people. Such understanding was not only the pillar of communist totalitarism, but it was one of the main (though not the only) causes of the crisis of that societies, and the central obstacle in overcoming that crisis. What was happening in Central and Eastern Europe was a victory for the people in their struggle for freedom and for the implication of fundamental human rights.

It was by no means inevitable that these developments would unfold in a linear fashion in the direction of free democracy, with a sound economic basis, which is a precondition for genuine stability. The reforms are irreversible. But the outcome of the ongoing process is still uncertain, even when the people involved there know exactly what the ultimate goal is towards which they are working. My notes attempt to shed some light on the subliminal contradictions between the intended results and the unintended consequences of the measures taken.

One most destructive challenge for the creation of the new societal order is the old boy's network of party cadres in Culture, Economy and Administration, which was not really abolished but has been "redirected." As a result of ideological targets, political loyalties, varied favors or extortionist commitment, the single-party system established long-term personal ties and dependencies on a large scale. The links extended into the most remote corners of society and above all of the apparatus of state, where the Communist nomenklatura generally existed beneath the headquarters level.[1] What is more, a major enzyme for its cohesion and loyalty towards the political system was its opposition to the Federal Republic of Germany, which represented a permanent challenge.

It was against this background that the last Communist government in East-Berlin after mid-November 1989 achieved on a substantial scale to cover up the destruction of the State Security Service ("Stasi") files incriminating the Communist regime against the opposition of the population and enabled to transfer considerable assets to Stasi members, which not only gave the recipients financial benefits but which also, in many instances, safeguarded positions of social power.

Ferdinand Kroh's analysis for eastern Germany in 1992 is representative to the East in general: "Wherever they can, former Communist power elites are taking hold of the 'economic foundation' by buying profitable companies and handing over the remaining mass of firms to the taxpayer. At the same time, like-minded comrades at the intellectual superstructure' level are not only ensuring that no public fuss is made about these activities, but also that the tremendous reconstruction attempts by the new democratic state and by the free and western-oriented market forces are presented as perfidious action against the people. The success of such power retention strategies by those who ruined the GDR under their rule impedes and jeopardizes the process of reconstructuring in eastern Germany."[2]

This leads to questions which still remain unanswered today: "To what ends will the forces trained in Communist conspiracy, strategy and tactics exert their influence? Is financial gratification the only aim? Will the Communist forces be willing to accept compromise and to demonstrate loyal cooperation, as observed among the former elites in other revolutions, or can a different code of behavior

---

[1] Vaclav Havel, in: Skyline Democracy, Kyklos Nicosia 1990, p. 2.

[2] Ferdinand Kroh, 'Cliques and Old Boy Networks': Power Detention Strategies of the Former East German Elite, in: Aussenpolitik, 2/1992, p. 147.

be expected in the case of the Communists?"[3]

The persistent re-naming of the revolution to "re-direction"/"change" ("Wende") by that forces, is an eloquent reflection of the longstanding efforts for legitimization which was practiced by representatives of the old regimes and which would not have been possible without the "Toleranz" of the citizens' movement.

In the fall of 1989, the need for theories existed, which, – freed from the East-West conflict – questioned the origin of the identity crisis, searched for criteria of new social ethics and demanded viable political ideas.

"In general, these groups reflected political currents of thought whose political goals and hopes were associated with the continued existence of the GDR with a reformed socialist-style system. Reforms were the main aspects. The revolution was a result, not the aim of activities during the take-off phase."[4] The revolutionary ambitions during this phase before 9 October 1989 were in large hindered by the different national self-awareness in West Germany. As Wettig summarizes: "Following the ideological revolution of he West German Left in 1968, there was often a conviction in the corresponding circles that the Germans should never again become a nation in view of their past national guilt. They had discredited themselves once and for all through their former national ambitions and had to expiate their guilt by renouncing not only a nation-state but also a national identity. Many leftists also took the view that the Germans should never again be allowed to exercise far-reaching decision-making powers. In some left-wing circles, therefore, the elimination of German nature became an undisputed postulate. Adding to the foreign policy goal on integration, those who held such views also postulated the domestic policy goal of creating a 'multicultural society'. An overlaying of German nature through alien components was regarded and encouraged by such circles as progress towards greater humanization. The envisaged de-nationalization of the Federal Republic of Germany was perceived as the prelude to the Europe- and worldwide elimination of 'national-narrow-mindedness' in general. Notions of this kind explained why some left-wing German intellectuals failed to understand and to accept the unification of their native country in 1989/90."[5] It was during

---

[3] ibid, p. 150; Cf. Benno Zanetti, Der Weg zur deutschen Einheit, Muenchen 1991 and Ehrhart Neubert, Eine protestantische Revolution, Berlin 1990.

[4] Helga Schubert at a forum discussion of the Adenauer Foundation, Magdeburg, February 7, 1993 (tape).

[5] Wolfgang Schuller, ibid.

this culmination phase of the revolution, which lasted about six months, from 9 October 1989 to 18 March 1990 that the German masses in the East insisted in the termination of the division of the country. It was their pressure "from below" which formed the policy and created history.

It is clearly evident that the reunified Germany has irrevocably become part of the West and that the dissolution of the Soviet empire could not change this in the least: it had not created the "Russian option". The only realistic question was where would the eastern frontiers of Atlantic civilization run in the future?

But what exactly is European identity? "To me, all those nations are European which were exposed during the course of their history to the three-fold influence of Athens, Rome and Jerusalem", Paul Valery declared in a famous lecture he gave in the Twenties.[6]

Today we would without hesitation also mention Celtic, Germanic as well as Slav roots, while the influence of the Arabic countries should not be ignored, either. And in this connection, would it be wrong to refer to the scientific and liberal approach, or to Romanticism and Socialism?

Precisely which Western values are basic to democracy? Inevitably the focus falls on the-set of values loosely called "individualism", however vague and even slightly pejorative the term may sound. Western democracy has been founded on a specific understanding of the individual as an autonomous being. This understanding means that the individual has a capacity for freedom, for realizing himself in the course of his actions, and that he has inherent rights over and against the demands of any community to which he may belong.

It is not very difficult to trace the source of these notions in the convergence of two cultural streams: the first originating in biblical religion, with Protestantism playing a decisive role in its application to political democracy; the second rooted in the Hellenistic view of man, transmitted to modernity via the Renaissance and the Enlightenment, and applied to the invention of democratic institutions by the French revolution and its successors.

But just as democracy is an idea that manifests itself in concrete institutions and social processes, so the autonomous individual is not only an idea but a lived experience. Actual human beings must feel themselves to be autonomous, to be free or aspiring to freedom, to have inherent rights.

---

[6]Paul Valery, in: Europäische Stimmen, Bonn 1963., p. 7.

Necessary are experiences through which these ideas and values become plausible in actual life. The fact that Western individualism has been challenged from within Western culture, notably by Marxism, complicates the situation. The unusual assumptions of Western individualism become sharply evident as soon as one compares them with what is taken for granted in the great majority of non-Western cultures, in all parts of the world, and indeed in the traditional substrata of Western societies as well, as in the remaining peasant cultures of southern Europe.

As Peter L. Berger states, "democracy is not a 'luxury of the rich', as has been argued; the rich, with or without democracy, usually manage to take care of themselves."[7] If democracy is indeed a political structure to safeguard the rights and liberties of the individual, it also happens to offer the most plausible structure for the protection of traditional values.

The state is not the only threat to traditional values. Other modern institutions and processes – the forces of the market and of technology, modern urban life, and mass communications – create their own threat.

The history of the European Union as an institutional mechanism of democracy shows that it not only allows but creates breathing space to traditional values and institutions. Only the democracy fosters pluralism and coexistence between modernized and more traditional sectors of society.

But what is essential to all this, democracy is the most practical method for safeguarding those "mediating structures" that are, themselves, the matrix of democracy.

Mediating structures are institutions that both give shape to peoples private identities and also help them relate to the large structures of a modern society. These institutions exist both in highly modern and in less developed societies, and they are very important in both. The most important of these are the family, organized religion and the structures of local community.

Others are such innovations as cooperatives, labor unions and other associations to protect or promote particular interests. Virtually everywhere, people have a strong interest in these institutions, because their most precious values and self-identifications are closely bound to them.

---

[7] Peter L. Berger, in: Dialogue, 2/1984, p. 8.

As we all have experienced in the past, totalitarian states, by their very nature, can not tolerate even the relative independence of such institutions; these must be leveled, controlled and integrated into the all-embracing policy. Six years after the "velvet revolution" the situation in the former communist states asks for a spirited Westernization of public life.

The lack of a more thoroughgoing democratic component within the all-European framework has meant that "there has been little discussion during more recent times about the meaning and the purpose of the EU"[8], as Prince points out. European integration was a product of an early post-war desire: "to preempt any recurrence of the kind of nationalist eruptions that precipitated the Second World War. This desire was melted together with the promise of prosperity for all to create the political and economic conditions that would reduce the likelihood of war. As a process of this post-war need for security and reassurance, the EU today is confronted by the fact that it no longer possesses the Wert an sich (self evident value) it once did; its appeal to a so-called post-materialist culture, spoiled by the expectation of prosperity and peace, has ebbed."[9] As the transparency of the European policy-making structures grows dimmer and the number of members grows larger, the greater will become for the cultures too the need to renew public commitment to the idea of Europe.

It is not so much the diversity of the sources of European cultural identity which is challenging, but rather the influence that such sources brought to bear on the principle of unity, that unity which is subliminally linked with this identity. Jacob Burckhardt formulated this as follows:

> "If, in largely intellectual matters, we do not feel we belong to this
> or that people, no longer to this or that country, but feel that our
> allegiance is to Western culture, then this is because the world was
> once Roman and all-embracing and the whole culture of antiquity
> has devolved upon us."[10]

A multifarious cultural identity has developed from this melting pot over the centuries and continues to flourish to the present day. And precisely here the great

---

[8] K. Michael Prince, Germany, Europe and the Dilemma of Democratic Legitimation, in: Aussen-politik, 1/1995, p. 14.

[9] ibid.

[10] Jacob Burckhardt, Europäisches Gut, Wien 1936, p. 12.

wealth of our continent is to be found. Far from preserving unchanged what has been attained, by fearfully retiring into a cultural shell, this multifarious cultural identity constitutes a factor of living and original synthesis that is constantly renewing itself. This kind of identity consequently emerges as the precondition for individual progress, group progress and the progress of nations. This identity stimulates and establishes a community of interest mobilizes inner reserves for action and provides creative adjustment from necessary changes.

Denis de Rougement emphasized this, as follows: "Each one of our cultures has to refine its personality, because fruitful dialogue is possible only between partners who are quite different and who know what they want, or who they are, or who at least passionately wish to fathom it. Nevertheless, none of our cultures, which have been personified this way, is an end in itself. Culture means just the totality of the means that are made available to people; they depend on culture in order to approach truth."[11]

Diversity – in values, in communication, in religion, in technology, in everything from politics to poetry – begins to replace uniformity. New institutions, from self-help groups and political splinter organizations to transnational agencies, spring up in the rubble of the democratization. The Western societies are "demassified" as Alvin Toffler prognoses already for the eighties. The political, economical and communication networks and bonds since the 1989 revolution develop into a global civilization on cross-nation and non-state base. It was Peter Brook who reminded us a year before the wall came down about this irresistible directions: "The valid truth is the truth of the moment. When many influences interact, through their converging rays, through their friction, a new view can emerge, fresh, surprising. (...) even within a single culture, each individual is conditioned by an ever wider mixture of global influences. As cultures intermingle (...), the audience is brought together before precise, yet universal truths."[12]

It is this challenge which enables a mutual respect of nations, their progressive cooperation, and their integration with the aim of a common management of problems. But the structure of current relations in Europe and the nature of their resultant problems can only be properly understood against the background of the historic changes brought about by the end of the Cold War. Overcoming the

---

[11] Denis de Rougement, in: Europäische Stimmen, Berlin 1990, p. 32.
[12] Peter Brook, World Theatre Day Message – March 27, 1988, flyer, US-Center of ITI.

factors of uncertainty which existed for decades and establishing a reliable and sustainable union between East and West does appear to be a real possibility. The challenge for culture today is how to use its anticipatory abilities. The dialectics of European identity shape the emerging outlines of the future.

Excerpt of a paper given at the 6th ISSEI-conference, 1998, Haifa, Israel; first published in the conference proceedings.

```
  BRECHT SOCIETY OF AMERICA
  59 S NEW
  DOVER DE 19901 20AM
```

```
  1-0001781051 02/20/90 TWX ESL62032161 DETA
  001 TDWX DOVER DE
```

► HEINZ-UWE HAUS
  C-O KLAUS SCHMIDT
  215 EAST EVERS
  BOWLING GREEN OH 43402

OPEN LETTER OPEN LETTER

WE SUPPORT THE EFFORTS OF THE DA PARTY, AND OF ALL DDR PARTIES AND FOR
GROUPS, IN DEVELOPING NEW, DEMOCRATIC STRUCTURES FOR ALL LEVELS OF
SOCIETY.
WE UNDERSTAND THE IMPORTANCE OF GRASSROOTS SUPPORT FOR GERMAN
UNIFICATION,
AND EXPRESS SOLIDARITY WITH THE STRUGGLE FOR A VIABLE COALITION IN THE
MARCH 18TH ELECTIONS. THE IMMEDIATE NEED IS OBVIOUS: A SOCIALLY
RESPONSIBLE
FREE ECONOMIC SYSTEM. BUT EQUALLY IMPORTANT, THE BUREAUCRATIC
STRUCTURES OF
GOVERNMENT MUST BE REFORMED TO ALLOW THE RE-ESTABLISHMENT OF INDEPENDENT
LOCAL CONTROL OF REGIONAL GEOGRAPHIC AREAS. SUCH GROUPS ALONE COULD
PROMOTE
AND IMPLEMENT ECOLOGICAL REFORMS IN MANUFACTURING, IN ENERGY CREATION,
IN
WASTE DISPOSAL--WATER DOES INDEED FLOW BOTH EAST AND WEST.
      HOWEVER, SPEAKING AS AMERICAN SCHOLARS AND PERFORMERS, CULTURAL
POLITICS IS ALSO A GREAT CONCERN. IN PARTICULAR, WE ARE TROUBLED BY THE
SLOWNESS OF THE INTERIM GOVERMENT IN DISMANTLING THE OPPRESSIVE
BUREAUCRATIC AND ADMINISTRATIVE STRUCTURES WHICH WERE SO CHARACTERISTIC
OF
THE FORMER GOVERNMENT. SUCH CHANGES ARE NECESSARY IF UNHAMPERED, FREE
DEVELOPMENT IN ART AND CULTURE IS TO BE ACHIEVED.
      THE RECENT EFFORT OF THE MINISTRY OF CULTURE, FOR EXAMPLE, TO ISSUE
"GUIDELINES FOR POLITICAL THEATRE" WOULD SEEM COUNTER-PRODUCTIVE. WHY
RESTRICTIVE "GUIDELINES" BEFORE THE ELECTION? SINCE THERE ARE NO
DEMOCRATICALLY ELECTED THEATRE WORKERS IN THE MINISTRY OF CULTURE, WHO
AUTHORIZED THESE STRICTURES? THE "THEATERVERBAND (VDT)"? BUT NOTHING
WHICH
OCCURED IN OCTOBER 1989 AND AFTER GRANTED SUCH POWERS.
      BUT PERHAPS MOST DISTURBING IS THE FACT THAT THESE SAME PEOPLE WERE
INSTRUMENTAL IN CREATING THE PROBLEMS THEY ARE NOW CLAIMING TO SOLVE.
WHO
BUT THEY ARE RESPONSIBLE FOR THE PAST YEARS OF MIND-EMPTYING STAGNATION
WHICH HAS PLAGUED THEATRE IN DDR AND STUNTED ITS RICH POTENTIAL FOR
EXPERIMENT AND GROWTH?
      WITH ALL HUMILITY, WE RECOGNIZE THAT WE ARE BUT DISTANT "FOREIGN
```

5241 (MM 10/89)
```

WESTERN UNION | MAILGRAM ®

OBSERVERS" OF THE POLITICAL PROCESS NOW UNFOLDING IN THE DDR; THAT THE PAIN
AND FRUSTRATION OF CREATING THE FUTURE MAY BE AS GREAT AS THAT EXPERIENCED
IN ENDURING THE PAST. PLEASE BE ASSURED, HOWEVER, THAT OUR CONCERNS ARE
GENUINE AND LASTING.

ABOVE IS A ROUGH DRAFT OF THE OPEN LETTER. PLEASE CALL WITH ANY COMMENTS,
CHANGES, IDEAS. WE WILL HAVE IT PRINTED AND READY FOR YOU WHEN YOU ARRIVE
IN PHILADELPHIA. BEST TO UTZ (COMPUTER EXPERT). FOR KLAUS: MY BITNET
ADDRESS IS:

(ADDRESS) XB.DAS@STANFORD.BITNET

(SUBJECT) [DDE1DS]DWIGHT

01:00 EST

MGMCOMP

11 Organization Proposes – Market Disposes

There is nothing new about innovation. History is the record of the human propensity to create, invent and solve. For what is new is an environment which has turned innovation into the first issue of the age. There are three familiar reasons for the urgency. First, State borders can no longer keep the outside world at bay. The interconnectedness of modern economies means that there is no hiding place from competition for companies, towns, regions or countries. Globalization has all but abolished the concept of the home market. Second, declining birth rates mean that Europe's economic burden is being borne by a smaller proportion of the population. This increases pressures on both the private sector (to increase productivity) and the public sector (to cut costs and find new approaches to service delivery). Third, the growing influence of the knowledge economy, fueled by dramatic advances in information and other technologies, is accelerating the pace of change. All three – the speed-up of time, the shrinkage of distance, and the graying population – feed back into an intensifying cycle of competition, with profound implications for employment, the quality of life and social cohesion. Unemployment in Germany is 12 percent. Few locations in Europe are better off. In these circumstances, innovation, or the successful exploitation of new ideas, can no longer be left to chance or the personal discoveries of great intellects. As a prerequisite of survival, it requires deliberate and systematic organization.

How can this be done? From the ongoing discussions emerged the outline of a new agenda for European innovation. It is based on a vision of a diverse and inclusive Europe in which the development of human capital is both a tool and an end. Underpinning this development is the concept of total innovation – innovation as a cultural attitude to a scenario of permanent change and of discontinuity, a guiding light not only for companies but also for universities and other knowledge producers, for the public sector and politics. The basis of innovation, whether in groups or in organizations, is the individual, and enhancing individual creativity requires innovative people management within organizations. Developing innovative practice across the board needs a supportive infrastructure of other institutions-notably European (de)regulation and research programs, government economic and scientific policies, and education. It needs a rich web of long- and short-term partnerships and alliances between them. Finally, the innovation agenda generates recommendations and guidelines for governments, academia, companies and not least individuals. (...)

No description of what innovation is means anything without a vision of what it is for. Although German politics continue to agree that a focus on deliverables is vital, a vision for European innovation is not an abstract luxury but the heart of the matter. Innovation is a process, and it needs fuel to keep it in movement. Since it is carried out by people not by market forces, a vision must supply the motivation which keeps them in the game. What should that vision be?

Some speak about 'filling the empty box of Europe'. When the machine is built, the single market completed, the common currency in circulation, what will be done with it? The EU members agree that Europe must add value to its human and knowledge capital, squaring the circle of economic development, social cohesion and political democracy. Investing in human capital is an instrument as well as an aim. On both counts it follows that innovation must be inclusive. All must take part; it cannot be left to 'experts'. Innovation is empowering, a means of taming change. It is also a responsibility. Finding new ways to use the accumulation of past research to meet the needs of the present may be Europe's most pressing practical need. One of the most important conclusions is that progress demands acceptance by every economic and social actor of the responsibility for change.

Innovation must also be diverse, answering to the needs of the citizens of the new Länder of Germany as well as those of Sicily or Wales. Diversity calls for a special mention here. Many people pay lip service to diversity and the linked notion of freedom of expression as competitive assets. They are certainly a vast potential source of strength-genetically, diversity is a driver of evolution, and given the fate of the command economies, Europe is fortunate in that it no longer believes in the illusion of control. But in practice there are few successful role models of managing diversity and contention, and in recent years many commentators have pointed to the economic outperformance of more homogeneous societies such as Japan and South Korea. The current turmoil in South East Asia is no cause for complacency. It is cause, however, for an urgent re-appraisal of Europe's rich differences as a key to unlocking innovation potential.

European innovation must meet other requirements. It must balance long and short term, public and private goods, basic and applied, national and local, spiritual and material. Europe's cathedrals represent the innovation of centuries, on a different timescale from those of politics or corporate economics. Modern Europe must respect these relativities and develop similar long-term commitments-a difficult political trick, as more than one speaker noted. Innovation in academia, the public sector and politics may be as important as that in corporations.

The aim in a society in which diversity is harnessed to generate superior innovativeness, sustained by policies and priorities which focus on human needs and human capital. This is easy to say. The key to making it actionable is to consider 'quality of life' not as an abstract entity but as a product and a market-something that people want enough to be willing to work and pay for. (. . .)

To fulfill the vision, any government should recognize that there is no Single Grand Theory of Innovation. The process varies by industry and size of firm, and is clearly influenced by different national cultures. It embraces change in products, processes, ways of organizing and managing people, small incremental improvements as well as significant step changes, and above all in ways of thinking.

The absence of a single model has implications for promoting 'best practice' – in this case best practice's learning how to learn to innovate better. Instead, the Red-Green Coalition boldly proposes a different concept: total innovation. Total innovation is not a methodology but an attitude of mind: a culture of mastering change rather than being a slave to it ("leading edge rather than bleeding edge," in one formulation). In a world of permanent change and discontinuity, total commitment to innovation paradoxically can provide the constant purpose which otherwise wavers in the flux. Total innovation is the acceptance that problem-solving and learning are an important part of the everyday responsibilities of individuals, companies and other organizations. They are not an optional tool or bolt-on. Innovation is what we do. (. . .)

As the first 100 days of the Red-Green Coalition shows, total innovation confronts head-on Europe's biggest innovation barrier: the risk-aversion which runs through its culture. Europe is over-regulated and unfriendly to entrepreneurship and small-form enterprise. Venture capital is underdeveloped. Individuals are less mobile and more conservative in their life-choices than in the US. Europe has a poor record of commercializing and marketing new technological ideas-witness the huge trade gap in IT and other advanced technology products. Companies, especially large international ones which compete for capital on world markets, tend to have a short-term financial orientation ('the quarterly results syndrome'). So do politicians focused more on European enlargement and monetary union than the collective competitive response. Preoccupation with short-term election results likewise does not sit naturally with a long-term concern for quality of life. (...)

Total innovation calls for a new understanding of risk. In what has been called the 'risk society', citizens daily must make choices (whether to eat beef, use sprays with CFCs, communicate with mobile phones or have unprotected sex) without the benefit of scientific certainty. So the idea of avoiding risk is meaningless. Progress itself manufactures risk, as in all those cases. While frightening, this is also liberating. Tradition is no longer an undiscussable guide to choice, and nor are 'experts'. Individuals must make up their own minds according to values as much as scientific evidence. After all entrepreneurship – "unreasonable conviction based on inadequate evidence," according to Tom Peters – is deliberate defiance of risk. For individuals, coming to terms with these choices requires new ways of thinking and behaving (innovation). If "freedom is the recognition of necessity" (Engels), innovation is freedom and empowerment.

For companies too, risk is an illuminating optic through which to view innovation. We all know, large companies in both Europe and the US are cutting back their research budgets. They appear to view research without immediate outcomes as a luxury which they cannot afford in times of intense competitive pressure. But this is to ignore its contribution to their future flexibility to innovate in response to new demands. In this perspective research is rather a form of scenario planning which companies cannot afford not to do. Putting it another way, research is a kind of "insurance against future surprises from the scientific and technological environment." This also goes for government or other publicly funded research. The payoff for basic long-term research, as for innovation generally, is as much in indirect educational results as in new products or processes. (...)

The innovation imperative also requires a refocusing of the role of companies and organizations within the economy. A successful economy contains both organizations and markets. The two are different and have different organizing principles. Markets are about efficiencies – getting the most out of existing resources, doing things at lowest cost. But they don't invent new resources. That is the job- and the uniqueness-of organizations. Organizations provide a (temporary) leeway from markets in which they can generate fresh value by developing new products and services and finding better ways of providing existing ones. Competitive markets then force the same companies to 'hand on' most of the value to others. The organization proposes, the market disposes. In this dance of co-evolution, companies and markets jointly drive the round of innovation which is the engine of economic growth.

Nevertheless, it is clear that total innovation must embrace European, governmental and the whole knowledge-producing and using infrastructure. Although neither Brussels nor national governments are drivers of innovation, they have a significant role as catalysts. On this principle, Europe should question the temptation to harmonize at all costs. It needs to achieve the same balance between the benefits of standardization and decentralized enterprise as companies. Standardization counterproductively damaging to local ingenuity at a lower level of intervention – for example, food. Europe should also concentrate on lowering the regulatory common denominator rather than imposing a new layer on national frameworks. Brussels needs to think innovatively itself about support policy. For instance, the experiences of the last ten years underscore the need for social-science/cultural aspects of innovation to be recognized as an integral part of the European Unification process rather than as a bolt-on extra. Nor can Europe avoid taking a hard look at competition policy. Although the idea of national champions is discredited, there may in some industries be a case for encouraging the formation of a single large European company to compete on more equal terms with global competitors. What governance structure should apply to such an entity is an interesting question for further discussion.

Excerpt from a draft for a lecture at the Cultural Foundation, Saenejoki, Finland, January 7, 1998.

12 No Longer Blown Backwards into the Future – About European Identity and the Storm of Progress

The socio-political paradigm change in 1989 indicates apparently also a rupture that inspires, even necessitates self-reflection. The inclusion of a wide range of diverse nations into the European Union in May 2004 is another challenge of the storm of progress. But is it not precisely the intellectual and political history of Europe that could teach us a strong distrust of shared identities in general and identities projected into the future in particular? To illustrate this point I would like to go back some 60 years in time to the year 1941 and to a German (Jewish) philosopher, Walter Benjamin. In this year, a few months before he committed suicide when his effort to escape from France threatened to fail, Benjamin wrote a short essay entitled *Über den Begriff der Geschichte*. Referring to a picture by Paul Klee, Benjamin evokes the famous and chilling image of the angel of history. This angel is looking back in horror towards the past. Where we see a long chain of events, the angel sees a terrible catastrophe, mounts of human misery piled upon each other and growing ever higher into the sky. She wants to kneel down at these heaps of misery, raise the dead and heal what has been torn apart. But that is impossible because a storm coming out of paradise blows straight into her wings and blows her backwards into the future while the heaps of human misery grow higher and higher before her horrified eyes. This storm, says Benjamin in conclusion, is what we call progress.

In the light of the many catastrophes that have since taken place in the name of national, ethnic, religious and ideological identities – in Auschwitz, in Hiroshima, in the Gulag-archipelago, in former Yugoslavia and in so many other places – we are forced to conclude that the angel of history has little reason to relax its horrified face.

It even seems as if the storm of progress that impedes her to kneel down and try to heal the wounds is accelerating both its pace and its force. Benjamin thought of the storm of progress in terms of the onmarch of instrumental rationality, culminating in modern industrialized societies that judge their own progress by their economical wealth and their technical control over nature – but close their eyes to the violence the suffering internally connected with this progress. The angel of history, however, does not close their eyes, as Europe's history teaches. She squarely faces the horror even while she is blown backwards into the future. To understand her courage in this respect better, we should take a closer look at the religious motives underlying the emotional and intellectual power of the image Benjamin evokes. Since the storm of progress is blowing out of paradise, a first and obvious religious motive is that of the fall. Seen in this light, progress appears as the movement away from the blissful situation in which man did not yet know fear and solitude and was not yet forced to try and control nature by means of the violent power of instrumental reason. However, apart from the motive of *the Fall*, there is also a second, very different religious motive at work in Benjamin's imagery, a motive that has a social significance for *European Identity*. The angel is clearly driven by compassion, by the impulse to wake the victims from death and heal their wounds. In this way the angel of history also symbolizes the higher capacities of mankind; she symbolizes a form of moral sensibility that is connected in the great world religions to divinity and presented to us both as admonition and as promise. The angel of history symbolizes this promise; she is capable of love and wants to console the victims, but progress blows her helplessly away into the future. Progress blows away love, we could conclude, and thus puts an end to history as an expanse of hope, not only the hope embodied in the spiritual message of the great religions but also the secularized promise contained in the great narratives of modernity. Postmodern history, the history of the ever expanding postindustrial society only seems to promise us more of the same: more consumption, more information, and more pollution, more lonesome autonomy and beyond that an intensifying struggle for increasingly scarcer resources on a worldwide scale.

This at least is the conclusion reached by many contemporary thinkers. Quite a few and certainly not the least important – like Fukuyama or Barzun – are motivated by a deep concern that such a black conclusion is indeed intellectually unavoidable. But maybe this conclusion is a little too hasty. Maybe it just exchanges the abandoned modernist belief in humanity and progress for an equally totalizing disappointment, for a deeply concerned and ethically motivated relativism that doubts everything except the truth of its own black diagnosis. Over and against such an uncritical postmodernism, Benjamin could remind us of the fact that the continuum of history as an expanse of violence and suffering should not be totalized. According to Benjamin, it is interspersed with moments of "Jetzt-Zeit", moments whereupon people are living in the here and now of shared hope and solidarity and contribute in decisive ways to practical learning processes, as Brecht would say. The idea of "Jetztzeit", of sudden leaps taking us out of the continuum of empirical history, brings me to a third aspect of the theme. Reflecting upon European identity, we not only remember our history and looking ahead towards its coming developments, but we are also engaged in *critique*, that is to say in forms of analysis that bring into play normative standards by which actual developments are judged in view of unrealized possibilities of a historical situation. Thus understood, critique is internally connected with hope, with the tenacious determination not to reduce history to a series of empirical events, but to judge and evaluate it both emotionally and morally in view of possibilities to lessen the suffering, to enhance the opportunities to experience joy and to increase the room people have to articulate what is most important for them and to increase the changes that they will be heard and understood by others.

However, does such a critical endeavor not confront us anew with the question of relativism and with the downfall of the great narratives? Does it not actually confront us with the question which standards to apply and how to justify them? And indeed, not only postmodern philosophers but also the modernist advocates of a critical, "Nachmetaphysisches Denken" ascertain that all sources of absolute knowledge and objective insight have either dried up or are so polluted that we should refrain from the seduction to find any certainty in them about our identity and our possible future. So to which standards could such a critical endeavor refer nowadays, other than the norms of a self-conscious intellectual sub-culture dressing itself up with the outdated garments of a European tradition having all but used up its utopian energy and spending most of its remaining intellectual power in the effort to undermine its former universal pretensions?

In 1989 we reached neither the end nor the beginning of history. But the democratic awakening of the Middle and Eastern European nations and its unifying force for the continent is the dominant quality and measure of today. From Estonia to Cyprus, from Wales to Silesia, in Athens and Prague count the same standards for critique and the normative justification for practical humanizing activities motivated by critical analysis and practical solidarity. It is the individual person and its unique worth that is at the centre of most humanist traditions of such different cultural roots. But then again: what is this individual person? How should we envisage its identity, characteristics and capabilities? In view of all that has been said already, it is clear that we can no longer meaningfully picture the individual person according to the modem model of the subject as a rational, self-contained, disembodied and autonomous person. It is precisely this humanistic and fallocratic model of the subject that has fallen prey to such a load of convincing critique during the division of Europe.

My central contention would be that Benjamin's model of the subject as a multiple entity has still a chance to enlighten, if it opens itself for the experiences, feelings and thoughts of a great many individuals in post-1989-Europe. In my opinion and experience, this practical, individualized and embodied humanism of the self-liberated social being also contains a promise. It is the promise that one day the angel of history will be able to do without wings, that it can become a human individual, no longer blown backwards into the future by the storm of progress but able to fold its wings and kneel down at the mounts of human misery. Not to heal what was broken, nor to restore a lost unity or fulfill a promised destiny, but caring for the victims and their wounds, not leaving them alone – and thus caring for and accepting his won wounds and multiplicity and for that reason being very much alive...

First published in Revista Brasileira, Rio de Janeiro, Brasil, Vol. 4, Nr. 12, December 2005.

13 Time of Parenthesis – Postmodernism and Christian Identity

We are living in a time of parenthesis, a time between eras, my friend Jacobos Kambanellis, the Greek writer, liked to say, when we discussed the Cold War "scenery" in the early 1980s. If man was not a thing, as declared by Erich Fromm, what companionship, then, could be found in that world? I had my experiences of communist totalitarism. Jacobos remembered his youth in Dachau, where he survived the Nazi camp, and Paris, where he studied Sartre, who documented how easy victim and executioner can change the role.[1] Today again, we have, in short, overwhelming moral reason but almost no cultural foundation for believing in ourselves. Our hearts fill with intense longing for heroic behavior, but our heads are loaded with pedestrian indoctrination about "conditioning". Our rhythm of existence is like a chain of opportunities. We must not be afraid of the contradictions between the intended results and the unintended consequences of the measures taken. Remember, the 1989 victory over the Soviet empire was not ending global struggle for freedom and democracy, as we know now-clearer than in the weeks of revolution. After all it was the great opportunity of Europe to re-start its engine for a challenging race worldwide.

While thinking globally, if we look to the EU the place to make a difference politically is still at the national level. Despite occasional outcries of postmodernist self-expression to the contrary, Westerners are capable and desirous of participating in political decisions to a greater extent than the present representative system permits. At the same time, the outcome of the ongoing processes is still uncertain, even if the people involved know exactly what the ultimate goal is towards which they are working. It is as though we have bracketed off the present from both

---

[1] Jean Paul Sartre writes in his review of Henri Alleg's book, The Question, which tells how the author, an Algerian journalist, was tortured by the French: "According to circumstances, anyone, anytime, will become either the victim or the executioner." In: MANAS Reprint, Vol. XXII, No. 3, January 15, 1969, p. 2.

the past and the future, for we are neither here nor there. We have not quite left behind the either/or of the past, but we have not embraced the future either. We have done (as always) the human thing: We are clinging to the known past in fear of the unknown future.

The question is how to outline an interpretation of that future in order to make it more real, more knowable. It is obvious, that those who are willing to handle the ambiguity of this in-between period and to anticipate the new era will be a quantum leap ahead of those who hold on the past. That's why one can draw the conclusion, that the time of the parenthesis is a time of change and questioning. Following the modern directions of Descartes, we believe in reason, and that human reason can grasp truths independent of time and place. The period in which we now live is often called "postmodernism". This view rejects that there are certain self-evident principles that may provide a foundation for other types of knowledge. According to Nancy Murphy[2] the use of the term in the Anglo-American world started some time around 1950. Others would perhaps say that postmodernism is something which evolved after 1968. But anyway, in 1979 Jean-Francois Lyotard published a book called *The Postmodern Condition.*[3] From then on the term is defined and the ideas of postmodernism have been much debated in the Western world. According to them, it is our possession of language that makes us human. Consciousness, thinking, and behavior have no source outside language. The slogan reads: "Reality does not determine language, language determines reality". This idealistic linguistic became the dominant paradigm for academic studies in the humanities and a powerful influence in the social sciences, and functions as major philosophical vehicle for secular humanism in the West.

For theatre makers from Aeschylus to Zuckmayer such propositions are undialectical and bizarre and have no "use value", as Brecht would say. But we are talking here about more than just academic fashion; we deal with hardcore "conditioning".

Postmodernism opposes Christianity, natural sciences, and all philosophies that give priority to natural science as a system of knowledge (including positivism). Christianity states that human nature and the human situation precede the gift of language. Kierkegaard, for example, strongly insisted that human nature de-

---

[2] Nancy Murphy, Anglo-American Postmodernity, New York, 1984.
[3] Jean-Francois Lyotard, The Postmodern Condition, Paris, 1979.

fines language, rather than – as postmodernism claims – language defining human nature. Natural science states that human nature exists, is biological, and is a product of Darwinian evolution by natural selection. Positive philosophies assert that science is the only valid investigatory procedure for determining objective truth. Postmodernism denies the existence of "truth" in any sense that would fit the preceding sentence.[4]

Postmodernism is associated with relativism, "anything goes". It is the position where one has left the belief in absolute truth, and instead embraces the idea that knowledge is dependent on one's perspective. Lyotard emphasized that in postmodernism one has left the idea of a grand narrative. In the Enlightenment, one had certain ideas guiding the culture, a unified project, where knowledge and information were important. In the Middle Ages, belief in God and the Bible gave society a grand narrative. All aspects of life could be interpreted from a religious point of view, and a large number of the population believed in God and Christianity. But in postmodernism, society is more fragmented. Belief in the One Truth, or universal criteria, has been substituted by a number of "small stories", and a diversity of criteria.

No doubt, the postmodernist succeeded to determine our time as one of multiple-option mood. If the megatrends[5] realize, such is the time, as one of the parenthesis, its challenges, its possibilities, and its questions. Although the time between eras is uncertain, it is a great and yeasty time, filled with opportunity. If we can learn to make uncertainty our friend, we can achieve much more than in stable eras. In stable eras, everything has a name and everything knows its place, and we can leverage very little. But in the time of parenthesis we have extraordinary leverage and influence – individually, professionally, and institutionally – if we can only get a clear sense, a clear conception, a clear vision, of the road ahead.

Another dogma of postmodernism is social constructivism. Whatever version we get presented the main idea again is that there is no objective knowledge or absolute representation of reality. No question, many of our concepts and categories are based on the social reality, and not because we veridically can represent physical reality. Not only theatre and religion reject mechanical materialism, common

---

[4] See Andreas Saugstad, Postmodernism: What is it, and What is Wrong With It?, North American Mission Board, January 25, 2001.

[5] John Naisbitt, Megatrends, 1982, p. 283.

sense and human experience, and last but not least science, train us, that reality is not created by social reality.

In short postmodernism indoctrinates in the following directions:

1. There is no objective truth (all knowledge, even formal knowledge, is relative to language systems).

2. There are no universal values shared by all human groups.

3. There is no predetermined human nature or human constants (gender, for example, is an existential language system construction).

4. Subjectivity (thinking, feeling, and self-conception) is the measure of all worth.

5. Personal confusion is the result of power of other persons over you (rather than, for instance, the result of invalid reasoning or factual misinformation).

The result, I repeat, of such teaching is pernicious. Such intellectual position is the basis for wholesale assault on, for example, principles of justice as embodied in the law in the Western democracies. In the Judeo-Christian understanding the individual is responsible for her own behavior; intentional killing is to be distinguished from accidental killing; punishment is based on a person's actions rather than their status – these principles, among others, are denied by strict postmodernism.

But living in our time of parenthesis, a time between eras, it is of crucial importance, that those stories we are exposed to, at the socio-cultural, religious, and educational levels, should be "inspiring, harmonious, peaceful and constructive ones, that open our eyes to the world, and that build and do not destroy".[6] For the promotion of a global multiculturalism as an urgently needed change from a culture of war to a co-existence in peace, postmodernism can be an ally.

Postmodernism rightly opposes utopianism; it reminds us of our great capacity to fail (Christians would include "sin" here) as well as to oppress "the other". Humans are prone to self-deception and rationalization. From a Christian point of

---

[6]Ada Aharoni, Global Multiculturalism versus the "War of Cultures", abstract for the GSPC-conference, Istanbul, June 23-27, 2004.

view, deep sinfulness prevents achieving earthbound utopias. One must be routinely self critical and wary of values opposing God's kingdom, which can easily creep into our minds. However, the key interpretive grid (hermeneutic) should not be, as Pope Benedikt told at his visit in Istanbul "one of suspicion, but of trust and charity, which enhances relationships with God and others".[7]

Postmodernism and Christian belief agree that one should appreciate cultural/ ethnic diversity rather than treating people as "other". Christians today are encouraged by their churches to show grace towards non-Christians since they themselves have been saved by God's grace. Colonialism, oppression, and slavery do not inevitably follow Christian belief. The Bible expresses sensitivity to the weak, the suffering, and the oppressed such as orphans, widows, and the alien. God Himself suffers with the human being (see Matt. 25:31-46; Acts 9:4). I remember Cypriot-Orthodox Archbishop Makarios, Church and state leader as well, reminding his people only months after the 1974 Turkish invasion of Cyprus and in the midst of a brute destruction of Byzantine heritage in the occupied territory: "Christians must show that their 'grand story' is both plausible and not inherently oppressive; rather, we are created by God to flourish when we are rightly related to him and others. Because we are recipients of God's grace, we have no right to think of ourselves as superior to non-Christians".[8] It was Makarios' goal to fight the demographic change and the "muslimization" through political means and not on religious terms. The co-existence of the islands inhabitants with their diverse religions, Christian-Orthodox, Roman-Catholic, Maronites, Jewish and Muslim, in one body of citizenship and European identity appeared to be a strong weapon to withstand Turkey's long term strategy.

Excerpt of a paper, presented at the 11th ISSEI-conference, Helsinki, Finland, 2008.

---

[7] Berliner Zeitung, Berlin, June 24, 2006.
[8] Heinz-Uwe Haus, Cypriot diary (unpublished).

14 Anti-Americanism

1   Some experts claim that today a virulent anti-Americanism is sweeping Western Europe – worse even than that during the Vietnam War, in the late 1960s and early 1979s, or the deployment of intermediate-range nuclear missiles in Europe in the 1980s. Only 36 percent of Europeans view U.S. leadership in world affairs as desirable. Markedly lower is their approval of the Bush administration: a dismal 17 percent. A majority of European say that the U.S. itself is the greatest threat to international security – more so than Iran or North Korea. Even before the fall of Saddam 57% of Greeks answered "neither" when asked which country was more democratic, the U.S. or Iraq. The memory of 9/11 has faded, and Western Europe looks at the global War on Terror as an exercise in propaganda foisted upon the innocent by conniving neocons.

But measuring anti-Americanism is an imprecise business. Though social scientists have tried for decades, distinguishing between an all-encompassing animus toward the country and its people on the one hand, and specific criticism of U.S. government policies on the other, have proven difficult. Anti-Americanism is less an critical attitude based upon both empirical evidence and an appreciation of history than it is an ideologically driven, oftentimes hateful outlook, characterized by a simplistic belief that American policymakers are mean-spirited, racist, and essentially evil.[1] We deal with an irrational aversion to a presumed "American character" and value system. A standard distinction between America-bashing and rational critique is that between disapproval of what America is and what America does. But the two inevitably become entangled during times of transatlantic friction.

2   For a brief moment after the fall of the Berlin wall, anti-Americanism seemed to have disappeared, especially in Germany, where decades of U.S. foreign policy – the 1948 airlift, Kennedy's 1961 "Ich bin ein Berliner" speech, Reagan's call

---

[1] Stephen Morris, "USA: A Valued Friend", The Australian October 23, 2003.

to tear down the wall – secured the 1989 peaceful revolution. The defeat of the Soviet system made America and the values of liberal democracy and free market economy the undisputed winners. The Left was for a short period in disarray. Yet the moment was brief, ending quickly with the onset of the 1991 Gulf war. The anti-American political subculture returned into the public eyes as a widespread peace-movement by not siding with the American-led coalition against Iraq, but with the occupier of Kuwait. In fact, that hostility grew throughout the course of the decade, providing the defining framework for European debates around an ever-shifting set of topical concerns: the Israeli-Palestinian conflict, the anxieties regarding globalization, international economic relations, and the efforts to develop an international agenda for ecological concerns. Berman observes as basic gestus an obsession: "No matter how the specific topic migrated, a discursive framework remained constant, always casting America as the fundamental source of discord".[2] Anti-Americanism is indicated precisely when reasoned argument gives way to sweeping generalizations and hostile innuendo, and the obsessive thought structures of prejudice and stereotype prevail.

And Berman underlines, that it was "precisely that vigorous anti-American subculture that made Germany such hospitable venue for Mohamed Atta and his terrorist partners as they prepared for the attacks on Washington, D.C., and New York. Yet, far from recognizing the European responsibility for having nurtured, harbored, and funded terrorists and terrorist networks, anti-Americans turn matters on their head, grotesquely blaming the United States for 9/11."[3]

3   The overwhelming majority of inhabitants of the communist empire had never a doubt, that the Soviet Union or Red China were predisposed to use force in obtaining their objectives on the world stage. (As a Berliner I witnessed the Stalin blockade of 1948, suppression of the 1953 uprise, then Krustshchev's Ultimatum of 1958 (the attempt of abolishing the Four Power status, converting West Berlin into a so-called free city and the withdrawal of the Western allies) or the erection of the Wall 1961.

When taken in conjunction with their presumed first-strike nuclear capability and their possession of the largest ground force on the globe, the sheer brutality

---

[2] Russel A. Berman, "Not Just Friendly Disagreement", Hoover Press, DPO HBERAE200, p. 31.
[3] ibid, p. 34.

through which the Soviet Union secured its post-war sphere of influence in eastern Europe led most in the American national security establishment to conclude that the Communist bloc was committed to the overthrow of the so-called 'Free World' through all means necessary.[4]

The Soviet intentions were indeed a commitment to the erosion of the free world influence through all means necessary, and that this design was deterred by the combined strength of the free world, led by the United States.

Lt. Gen. Pacepa, the highest-ranking intelligence official ever to have defected from the Soviet bloc writes about the communist strategy: "The European leftists, like any totalitarians, needed a tangible enemy, and we gave them one. In no time they began beating their drums decrying President Truman as the 'butcher of Hiroshima.' We went on to spend many years and many billions of dollars disparaging subsequent presidents: Eisenhower was a war-mongering 'shark' run by the military-industrial complex, Johnson as a mafia-boss who had bumped off his predecessor, Nixon as a petty tyrant, Ford as a dimwitted football player and Jimmy Carter as a bumbling peanut farmer. In 1978, when I left Romania for good, the bloc intelligence community had already collected 700 million signatures on a 'Yankee-Go-Home' petition, at the same time launching the slogan 'Europe for the Europeans'."[5]

No doubt the final goal of the anti-American offensive was, as Pacepa underlines, "to discourage the U.S. from protecting the world against communist terrorism and expansion". The old KGB hand tells it: "Sadly we succeeded. After U.S. forces precipitously pulled out of Vietnam, the victorious communists massacred some two million people in Vietnam, Laos and Cambodia. Another million tried to escape, but many died in the attempt. This tragedy also created a credibility gap between America and the rest of the world, damaged the cohesion of American foreign policy, and poisoned domestic debate in the U.S."[6]

The New Left, heavily influenced by Marxist ideology, portrayed during the Cold War the Soviets on the defense and American "aggression" as responsible for struggles of the post-war era. As one commentator has remarked, the New Left argument was one that could be best interpreted as "an ongoing function

---

[4]See John Lewis Gaddis. We Now Know: Rethinking Cold War History. (NY: Oxford University Press, 1997)

[5]Ion Mihai Pacepa, Propaganda Redux, *The Wall Street Journal*, August 7, 2007.

[6]ibid.

of America's capitalist political economy ... whose structural dynamics required both ever-expanding markets for a continuous flow of surplus goods and capital and easy access to raw materials in a freely trading world". The New Left claimed that the American commitment to Europe after World War II was more about the securing of markets for the American capitalist economy – and thus an end in itself – than it was a means of defending the 'Free World' against the Soviet Union.[7]

4   Many Cold War critics are victims of irony and some of the most vociferous critics of perceived American moral superiority have themselves been supporters of or apologists for dictatorial regimes. As one commentator as recently pointed out, "those leaders of the moratorium marches against the US during the Vietnam War had little to say about the fate of human rights in Indochina after the communist victories."[8] They were driven by a profound and blanket dislike of anything the United States does at any time.

From Australia's Labor ministers like Tom Uren, Clyde Cameron and Jim Cairns to California's Hollywood entertainers like Barbra Streisand a wide range of naked apologists for the dictatorships in both Vietnam and China dominated the public discourse in the West. The same is true for American intellectuals. Noam Chomsky spent much of the 1970s denouncing the Carter administration for its human rights policies, and tried ardently to discredit reports of massive human rights violations in Vietnam and a holocaust in Cambodia. 'Not in our Name', a U.S. wide 2002 "project", again spearheaded by Chomsky and affiliates, was part of this resentment. At one late-October march in Washington, there were signs proclaiming "I love Iraque, Bomb Texas" and depicting President Bush wearing a Hitler mustache and giving the Nazi salute. At the risk of over-dramatization, one sees the point of a recent commentary that, when viewed in these terms, Chomsky, like his anti-American cult followers, is "a Stalinist wolf in libertarian sheep's clothing."[9]

Homegrown hostility to American society and the American experiment is hardly a new phenomenon, but in the 19th century it tended to be limited to

[7] See William Appleman Williams. The Tragedy of American Diplomacy. 2nd ed. (NY; Dell, 1972).
[8] Editorial, "Odd Priorities of US-bashers", The Australian, October 28, 2003
[9] Stephen Morris, a.a.O.

tiny and insulated elite circles (see the writings of Henry Adams). Now, it is a calling card for tens and hundred of thousands who share rare material splendor. That brilliant trio of Roman imperial writers, Petronius, Suetonius and Juvenal, warbed about such *luxus* and its effects upon the elite of their era, among them cynism, nihilism, and a smug and crippling contempt for one's own.

Western Europe's anti-Americanism is fed by this moral relativism (some call it "Bush Derangement Syndrome") of some U. S. writers, actors, athletes and academicians, who reveal in their statements less a liberal attitude than a habitual self-absorption. The novelist Philip Roth complained that the U.S. since 9/11 had been indulging itself in "an orgy of national narcissism", although he also conceded, reclaiming his title as the reigning emperor of aesthetic narcissism, that immediately after the fall of the Twin Towers New York "had become interesting again because it was a town in crisis' – a fleeting, final benefit to connoisseurs of literature from the death of thousands."[10] Another writer, Alice Walker, speculated weather Osama bin Laden's "cool armor" might not be pierced by reminding him of "all the good, nonviolent things he had done."[11] Traveling abroad, the actress Jessica Lange pertly announced: "It makes me feel ashamed to come from the United States – it is humiliating".[12] Tennis celebrity Martina Navratilova, who has earned millions from corporate sponsors, castigated the repressive atmosphere of her adopted homeland, a country whose behavior is based "solely on how much money will come out of it."[13] Hanson summarizes the observations as phenomenon: "There was the well-known poet who forbade her teenage daughter to fly the American flag from their living-room window, the well-known professor who said he was more frightened by the speech of American officials than by the suicide-hijackers of 9/11, and the well-known columnist who decried our 'belligerently militaristic' reaction to the devastation of that day".[14]

5   The Italian historian Federico Romero argues there is something deeper here at work than simple disillusionment with U.S. policies – and it's not anti-Americanism. He argues the transatlantic estrangement is the product of a cultural and

[10] Victor Davis Hanson, 'Bomb Texas', The Wall Street Journal, January 13, 2003.
[11] ibid.
[12] ibid.
[13] ibid.
[14] ibid.

social parting of ways that began with the Cold War's end. During the East-West conflict, there existed a consensual view across the Atlantic of what "the West" and "Western" meant – in terms of shared values, institutions, and procedures. This cultural hegemony was largely dictated by the United States, a result of Europe's postwar weaknesses.

The end of the Cold War not only altered Europe's strategic dependence on Washington but also decoupled Europe from the U.S. as an economic model, a cultural Mecca and political beacon. This process was abetted by ongoing social changes in Europe and the U.S. that further accentuated those differences in religious attitudes, demography, wealth distribution and migration patterns. This shift, argues Romero, is due largely to Europe's own self-perception as adherent to a "European social model" based on ideas of collective solidarity, secularism, welfare state practices, pots-nationalism and environmental responsibility. This model sells itself as more just and effective than the American one. Paul Hockenos hopes for the best, when he says: "Likewise, it is not blind anti-Americanism but European preferences for soft power, multilateralism and international justice that have resulted in more autonomous EU security policies".[15] It speaks for itself, that states like Spain and Germany developed the strongest voices in this direction.

But I would rather side with Berman's central claim, that anti-Americanism is not a response to American policies, American influence, or any broader process of "Americanization". Western Europe had very different experiences of American reality – from ally to occupying force – and none is the real matter. It is also obvious, that the Communist camp (as well as the Right wing ideologues) have their share, but are not the essential force to keep the movement going.

Berman reminds us of deep and hidden motivations: "Anti-Americanism ... is a cultural mentality that, emerging long before the rise of American power in the early twentieth century, is a reaction against the very presence of America in the world. The European discovery of the new world upset the traditional European world view, with Europe self-confidently at the center. Indeed, ever since the so-called first contact of European travelers with the inhabitants of the new world, Europeans have expressed anxieties regarding the brute nature, the presumed absence of history, and an undifferentiated homogeneity imputed to

---

[15] Paul Hockenos, "Conflicting Visions", *The Atlantic Times*, May 2008.

the western hemisphere."[16]

These are precisely the standard tropes of Anti-Americanism, an ideology with a long past, replete with stereotypes that are regularly recycled in new historical circumstances.

A German discourse of anti-Americanism became prominent, at the latest, in the early nineteenth century as romantic authors like the poet Nikolaus Lenau increasingly described the United States in pejorative terms, associated with their negative judgments on both its capitalism and its democracy. Aesthetic attitudes of cultural elitism have here their roots. Modernization = Trivialization, the notion of America as lacking high culture, "American quantity" versus "European quality", in short a nostalgia for the golden age of a premodern world has turned into a widespread hostility particularly in the cultural sector.

In contrast, the towering German author of the age, Johann Wolfgang Goethe, repeatedly expressed admiration for the young American republic. His opposition to the romantic antimodern reaction indicated the initial phase of a positive German attraction to America and the values of modernity associated with the American Revolution. "The deep, competing currents of pro-American and anti-American perspectives in German culture, in other words, are quite old, which underscores why German anti-Americanism cannot be explained away as a friendly policy dispute or even as a response to aspects of the role the United States has played in Germany in the twentieth century", states Berman and concludes, "thus, it is not anything that the United States does to Germany, no recognizable Americanization, that elicts anti-Americanism."[17] In his view it is the mere fact of the presence, in the world, of a society defined in terms of capitalism and democracy that scandalizes sectors of German and old European society. It is not an intrusive imposition of America's democratic capitalism that provokes the protests but the mere temptation that it represents.

"Pretending to oppose American power, anti-Americanism is in fact the ideology of opposition to the democratization of politics and the liberation of markets".[18]

Here the communist anti-Americanism still focuses on foreign policy disputes

---

[16] Russel A. Berman, ibid, p. 38; see Suzanne Zantop, Colonial Fantasies: Conquest, Family, and Nation in Precolonia Germany, 1770-1870 (Durham: Duke University Press, 1997), pp 18–42.

[17] Russel A. Berman, ibid, p. 40.

[18] Russel A. Berman, ibid, p. 39.

from the Cold War era: Vietnam, Cuba, Chile, Nicaragua, and so forth.

"Postdemocratic anti-Americanism" calls Berman currant complaints that the US remains reluctant to surrender elements of their sovereignty in order to transfer them to international bodies. Advocates of forms of international governance oppose the American insistence on national independence as a precondition for the democratic expression of popular will.

6   The point is that the principles objectified in the American Revolution have proven to have universal appeal because they speak to basic aspects of the human condition everywhere.

"Here or nowhere is America", spoke Goethe's Lothario in the novel *Wilhelm Meister's Apprenticeship*. By this he meant that the political and social revolution of democracy, initiated in the American Revolution, ought to be pursued in Germany, and not primarily through German emigration to the United States.[19]

For Goethe, the structure of emancipation – democratic government and free market – modeled in the United States was worthy of emulation elsewhere. It is that potential of freedom in human history that anti-Americanism resists.

Excerpt of a paper presented at the 11. International Conference of the International Society for the Study of European Ideas (ISSEI), University of Helsinki, Finland, July 28 – August 2, 2008.

---

[19] Johann Wolfgang Goethe, *Goethes Werke*, ed. Erich Trunz (Hamburg: Christian Wegener Verlag, 1962), VII, p. 431

15 About Capitalism

Today's economic meltdown is complex. So will be the decision making. But instead of dealing with the dialectics of the events bizarre "reality"-sideshows entertain the audience and waves of populist judgment are working their way through its minds. An old exorcism has returned: Capitalism is under siege, its future unclear.

In anticipation of this week's G-20 summit last Sunday's New York Times (March 29, 2009) reports that "Mr. Obama will confront resentment over American-style capitalism and resistance to his economic prescriptions when he lands in London. ... (He) will be tested in face-to face meetings by the leaders of China and Russia, who have been pondering the degree to which the power of the United States to dominate global affairs may be ebbing. ... The American banking collapse, which precipitated the global meltdown, has led to a fundamental rethinking of the American way as a model for the rest of the world." I agree, the world is sick and tired of America's patronizing know-it-all attitude.

The newspaper forecasts what most probably will influence the diplomatic dialogue. It expresses concern about the enormous difficulties the interwoven economies of the world are facing. But the report also sides with what I witness this week through PBS and BBC on the streets of the financial district of London: capitalism-bashing.

From my work as theatre maker I know, that attitude and gestus tell the story, not just the words. Unfortunately, in the present mediathon environment, drama without contradictions counts more than judicious journalism. Clear-cut "evil-doers" and their opposites are prized over ambiguous characters who do not wear either black or white hats. Once-definable distinctions between truth and fiction are blurred more than ever before. A gestus of witch-hunting seems to taint the facts that come to light. But that is as misleading the public as the common anti-American agitation, which, as we see, has re-arranged its vocabulary since Obama's presidency.

The understandable anger about greed and wrong doing on Wall Street should not be used for self-righteous indignations, as executed in the hearings or comments about AIG.

The outcome of the populist backlash may not be benign.

"I am angry," the president said last week. "What I want us to do, though, is channel our anger in a constructive way." But that may require confronting the close relationship between big business and mainstream politics that stimulated the original Populists into action. Over the past two decades, AIG has donated more than $9 million to congressional candidates; Obama's own campaign war chest was stuffed with checks from a variety of corporate figures, as well as smaller amounts from middle- and working-class people. Such inconsistencies cry for dialectical narration! When less than 5 percent of Americans say they have "a great deal of confidence" in Wall Street, it may be perilous to retain a Treasury secretary who has spent a good deal of his career around the same financial industry that now needs regulation. In the theatre, where we enjoy such contradictions as source of instruction, knowledge and enlightenment, we are aware, that there is always a main contradiction that plays the leading, decisive part; the rest are of secondary, subordinate significance. How are the new protagonists at the White House "dialecticizing" the events?

People may feel in their anger to be surrounded by Wild West unregulated capitalists, but what they really should care for is policy-making to control the behavior. What we need to restore to the present debate is logic, not anger; principles, not wrath. "Some of the demonstrators in this week's G-20 protest jamboree are demanding the 'overthrow' of capitalism. Well, there are lots of things that can be done to 'capitalism' – it can be undermined, suppressed, sabotaged, even outlawed – but it cannot be 'overthrown' because in itself, it has no power," Janet Daley writes in the London Telegraph at the same day as the New York Times reports its populist worries. The author clarifies: "It is the very opposite, in fact, of tyranny. It is simply the conglomeration of all the transactions made between individual and corporate players in an open market. Some people may gain power through those transactions but that power is transient and contingent on their own financial success: They are not installed in immutable positions from which they can be forcibly removed in a coup d'etat." The question we are wrestling with now – and which the G-20 will certainly fail to resolve – is, as the writer puts it, "how much the bodies which actually do have power should undermine, suppress, sabotage or even outlaw the practice of capitalist exchange." We hear from the summit in London, that all governments agreed to boost business — to be capitalist or not was not the question.

"Those who talk of 'overthrowing' capitalism are determined to depict it as a system of government in a precise parallel with socialism, when in reality, capitalism is not a system in the ideological sense. It is, if anything, an anti-system: the aggregation of human behavior as it goes about fulfilling particular wants and needs. It can be described in anthropomorphic terms, such as 'ruthless' or 'benign' but of itself has not motives and no objectives." The author touches here a most important point: people are wrong, that markets need to have 'values': only people have values, methods of exchange do not. The populists' rhetoric avoids such differentiation. Janet Delay summarizes her argumentation as follows:"It is in the interests of the Left to talk as if capitalism and socialism were ... analogous because then they can be seen as competitors and in bad times, the command economy as opposed to the market-based one can win the popularity contest. But this fallacious argument into which... a great many well-intentioned people are allowing themselves to be drawn is very dangerous: capitalism isn't really an 'ism', which is why the term 'free-market economics' is so much more apt."

As someone, who has experienced for 45 years not only communist social and political dictatorship in general, but its inherent command economy too, I also wonder, how after all short-term-politics would fixate on "capitalist flaws" – instability, unemployment, inequality – instead on the necessary tools for economic success. The cultivation of anti-capitalist feelings is as dangerous as the terrorists' jihad against the West. Any direction has to be aware, that the free world is a minority on a globe of non-democratic regimes. The global economy may help to balance political coexistence but it is not a free ride.

The actual reality is just too blatant to be ignored.

Newsweek argues in this week's cover (March 30, 2009), the problem with populist rage – defined as "the discernible public feeling that the few are unjustly profiting at the expense of the many" – is that while it is cathartic, it can lead to bad decisions that may make the situation against which one is raging even worse. This does not have to happen: as Robert J. Samuelson points out, "Great reform waves often proceed from scandals and hard times". The Great Depression gave the U.S. deposit insurance; mortgage guarantees helped build after World War II the middle class. The test of the moment is whether "our political and commercial leadership can restore credibility to the institutions of capitalism (which are the creators of wealth and a source of democratic strength) that have to come to grief." The risk at the moment is that understandable anger over the paying of publicly funded bonuses to people who self-evidently failed to perform well – if they had, they would not need public funds – could, as Samuelson writes, justify "punitive taxes, widespread corporate mandates, selective subsidies and more meddling in companies' everyday operations."

Let's hope, that the administration soon regrets its interventions. The credit crisis will pass and the auto overcapacity will sort itself out one way or the other.

As experience teaches, government cannot create prosperity. The best government that government can do, and the aim to which it should direct its efforts, is to create the conditions under which individuals can prosper. As the history of the U.S. proves, the way government does this is by promoting and maintaining individual liberty through limited constitutional means. It is individual liberty – not government – that is the engine of prosperity.

When future Americans look back on this period and ask "What was going on" the cultural context of the early twenty-first century may explain at least as much as the characters and the official actions that played out against that backdrop.

April 4, 2009

16 Cultural Memory and Theatre Work: Personal Reflexions

Linking my artistic thinking with training and teaching is, moreover, the attempt to ascertain the fragmentary and apodictic aspects of my awareness and to find an appropriate form of expressing them. It enables me to reflect on my own aesthetic, societal and political experiences and to use them under interdisciplinary and transcultural conditions. It confronts me compellingly with my won national and cultural identity: enabling me to affirm it, understand it, learn from it, yes, enabling me to cultivate it, in order, eventually, to be able to act from an absorbed, modified, new historical awareness. Some annotations to this, briefly sketched.

1   Since Thespis went before his fellow citizens, insights and evaluations have been the result of alienation of what is too close. It is the reading of a story, according to what Brecht makes us experience, that brings the audience into play. The fable, as we know, develops from the performance: it is not the illustrated synopsis of what has been written down.

In my case the experiences and observations from early childhood – at the end of the war in 1945 and the years after that – have become a kind of dramaturgical counterinsurance with regard to perception and description of social reality. It appeared to me as if the nation had lost the unity of action. Even the so-called hour zero did not stop at the ramp. The fourth wall was as worn out as the people and the country. The horrors of the Hitler regime had to be recorded in order to make visible the causes of the hardships that followed. At the same time we had to assume that they did not pre-determine the regime unavoidably, but that they did generate it and made it possible. Under the given political conditions it became clear to me very early on that, and how, social processes change cultural practices and contents of consciousness of the community and of individuals.

What is described today as "cultural transformation", appeared to me neither then (when the outcome of allied occupation of my native country appeared thoroughly open) nor later (during the sheer hopelessness of the Cold War) as a "phenomenon of natural history" (as, for example, predominantly accepted by German literary historiography into the 1960s), but appeared to me to be agreed upon, voluntarily, between generations, in brief: "product of negotiation" (which it has been understood to be more recently). As such it has to do with a common denominator of world view, far into the cultural past and across time.

Why this appeared to me, born in 1942, so unquestionably self-evident, why it has become more important at every instance of retrospection, that I refer to it at every opportunity that presents itself to me, is surprising only if you disregard the German tradition of reflecting the past. An example from the Romantic period: I am convinced that Schlegel and Tieck's translation of Shakespeare would have been less successful in the people's political imagination without the preceding collection of fairy tales by Musaeus. The renewed despotism could be interpreted as liberation from national socialism only by cynics. The heteronomy of Soviet ideology mobilized the unspoilt, the upstanding and the honest among old and young, not to fall again for lies and deception.

The term "generation" has nothing to do, already for Dilthey, with arithmetic that balances age groups or periods of time against alternation of generations. Dilthey already speaks of the "naturally inner measure of time ... in relation to spiritual movements."[1] A generation forms "a tight circle of individuals, who, by means of dependence on the same great facts and changes, as they appear in the age of their receptivity, are united into a homogenous whole, despite the heterogeneousness of factors that come into it."[2]

Generations are thus defined through the context of their experience. A generation can therefore comprise people of very different ages, and a year group can lead to several generations. If that is understood and experienced, it provides security from deterministic rigidity. Historical awareness thus includes free choice of cultural identity, yes, well-nigh demands it as a means to the end. With regard to theatre work, such an understanding of culture activates, as memory, the processes that Brecht integrates under the term of "intervening thinking".

It appears to me indispensible in actor training, for the understanding of the

---

[1] Wilhelm Dilthey, Die geistige Welt, Gesammelte Schriften, Bd. 6, 1. Hälfte, Hsg. V. Karlfried Grueder, Stuttgart 1957, p. 42.
[2] ibid. p. 37.

dramaturgy of plays, in directing, in every form of making theatre, to ascertain one's own origin, the similarities, and the aspects that are repeated over generations, in order to achieve a topical historical awareness and to represent on that basis the dialectics of scenic events.

2 Descriptions are never innocent. They intervene in the described and change and form it.

In particular at critical points in time that make individual elements of cultural heritage appear obsolete, it is essential to "problematise" customary understanding of the world and to evoke "struggles of interpretation" within collective memory. Cultural studies research by now agrees that every cultural transformation on the level of social institutions and groups goes along with techniques and modes of remembering, all in line with Halbach's succinct explanation that "societal thinking is essentially a memory".[3]

This, let's call it pointedly "sociology of memory made social" was realized exemplarily in Brecht's handling of the dialectics of objection. This is what made the early productions of the Berliner Ensemble – *Mother Courage* (1949), *Caucasian Chalk Circle* (1952) to *Galileo* (1956) – into high publicity events. Brecht champions contexts of experience – of before and after 1945 – as "strategy from below", for "brains of tomorrow" – resisting what is there.

Actors such as Thomas Holtzmann in Kaiser's *From Morn to Midnight* (at the Schillertheater) or Gisela Uhlen and Herwart Grosse in Ibsen's *Nora or A Doll's House* (at the Deutsches Theater) gave me as an adolescent an idea of and an incentive to the possible horizon of our art – beyond ideological encroachment. Jessner and Reinhardt's raison d'être could not be disposed of after the hour zero, Gustaf Gründgens and Wolfgang Langhoff's aesthetic discipline had more in common than their political biographies may lead to believe.

No matter how unreliable imagination and its sibling, since the 18th century, memory, may be, the associative creation of analogies between past and present can be identified as the source of all narration. Whether on the Greek orchestra or from the pageant wagon, on the baroque stage or with the help of the Brecht-curtain – the audience and the performers are together negotiating the events and

---

[3] Maurice Halbachs, Das Gedächtnis und seine sozialen Bedingungen, Berlin, Neuwied 1966, p. 390.

allow each other their subjective spinning of tales. It is always the play with the changeability of the given, which in the end does not know either perpetrators or witnesses, but conspirators. According to Schiller's encouragement – "thoughts are free" – in the theatre the whole multiplicity of philosophical and political interests has to be reckoned with. That's why it is so important to be always alert that not the words make the difference, but the gestus that is at their basis. The situations to which the representations refer are stored in the spectator's memory. If he sees only a hint to them on stage, he becomes aware of them, he brings them to the stage, and in most cases unexpectedly he moves on to the issue that concerns him. Under the conditions of dictatorship this is much stronger and much more frequently the case than in a democracy, where often mock attacks laze away the seriousness of the situation (From I to me, that's the wrong kind of empathy.

3   Gottfried Benn writes: "Only when you get old you know much you need mental support, the pointers, the thoughts of the past, the motives reaching back."[4]

The poet notes this in 1944 – in inward emigration, as physician with the Wehrmacht at the front. In this he touches thoughts also of those who grew up in post-war times, who also experienced how exacting it is for artists to measure, illegally, the changeability of what is there, while at the same time spreading silence over what is yet unfinished. In my case the replacement of the Nazi-regime by a Soviet-communist dictatorship in that part of Germany in which I grew up, was the backdrop that always remained in view of the events that had to be represented. Insights and valuations are constructed through achievements of memory. It is an imperative of fairness and honesty to acknowledge that poetry – in the German theatre the cardinal form of cultural memory – is essential in understanding what is one's own. That history is not a process to realize ideology and ideals, but, as Benn puts it, "that together to prevent the grossest of events, is the only possibility that is directed against it"[5] has moulded over decades of German and European separation the consciousness of my generation. This is the main characteristic of my cross-generational self-determination.

Klopstock's odes and the action of the Graf Stauffenberg 1944, the courage of Blücher and the nature poetry of Huchel, hope and death of Imre Nagy 1956 and

---

[4]Gottfried Benn, Ausdruckswelt, Verlag Ullstein GmbH, Frankfurt/Main – Berlin, Ullsteinbuch Nr. 494, 1962; p. 34.
[5]ibid. p. 44.

Jan Palach 1968, the legacy of Opitz, the patriotism of Fichte and target-oriented politics of Pope Paul II were self-liberating contexts of experience and survival; they are cultural memory of a voice that formed people, a voice my year group wanted to hear. That's why the conflicts of the years of European separation found an end almost without a struggle. The flow of language was in silence. The fall of the Wall almost twenty years ago and the return to Europe brought language and concepts back to light as if by mutation. "We are the people. We are one people", the demonstrators chanted in the streets in 1989. My production of Hamlet at a West German municipal theatre at the same time was under the motto of Freiligrath, "Hamlet is Germany". The appropriate interpretation and appropriation of what has been experienced is what is due to the spectator's emotional memory and interests. It is always dialogue and relationship, moving and in its best moments of prophetic urgency.

4   Making theatre attracted me as a child, because it appeared like a shelter, in which the oppressed human being could climb from bondage to perfection and beauty. The stage appeared well-nigh as the reversal of the experienced suppression. Theatre immunized against the day-to-day indoctrination. Shakespeare, Goethe, Schiller, Ibsen, Wedekind and Brecht kept reality at bay to the extent that I learnt to evaluate it calmly.

Even a lost so-called "socialist-realist work", in which I had to act occasionally during my first engagements, offered chances against the sparseness of life outside the theatre, because you were always secretly agreed with the audience to get the potemkinesque conditions going at least in the head.

Above all, however, the classics taught us to point beyond adversity and time. Through them I was always able to see my activity as the power to glorify change and transition. They taught faithful service and "techne", technical and manual mastery of their art as well as ours. This alone was both: weapon and secret of the banned ideals. To those who eat of the forbidden apple once, God opens the entire world (Thus or in a similar way Aristotle's motto would be rendered in Paul's language to allow it to apply today, too).

Hölderlin's striving for the "highest beauty" became equally familiar to me – at least the more often I recited him and sought to fathom his "complete experience of God" – as Toller and Borchert's expressionistic screams after the two World Wars. In brief: a world that murders the heart, stifles virtues and paralyzes the spirit of youth, was only too familiar for me. Of course I was not sure at all that the historical world was supposed to follow the world of ideas, to affiliate to it or to even notice it. However, I was, precisely because of literature and poetry, convinced "that the world of ideas has to apply its yardstick to the world of history. To apply means: to express it, formulate, illuminate, group it."[6]

Creating expression determines appearance, interlaces it with the here and today. The societal niche of theatre was in this regard both a transcendental act (in which everyone is free to open up to it), and an inner scaffold that binds the contents, experiences of images and thinking, the "illegal" thought processes about covered unity (Brecht calls this gestus). The ability to handle the word in its dialectiv, i.e., as social opposition, presupposes thinking that secures form. Causality is, in this context, only a very meager process of attribution. To bind language as relationship, thought, image, sound and rhythm, as process in the scenic context and to confront them with the interests of the spectator was, politically, rather in the mode of Schweyk rather than really showing courage.

5   I am convinced the early cultural imprint is a spring of creative power for life.

Every now and then, when I am weary of the English because my ability to fathom it increases the longer and the more on a daily basis I live with it, I return to my mother tongue, as if to ascertain my world of expression. In my American office I then search, like an addict suffering from withdrawal symptoms for the few treasures of my home literature. Again and again for Luther's translation of the New Testament, Goethe's Faust, Hölderlin's poems. The slim Reclam volume No. 7857/58 *Deutsche Minnesang* and Wolf Biermann's *Fünf Briefe aus gegebenen Anlässen*, published by Zweitausendeins, are also among them. These days they are Gottfried Benn's essays and Golo Mann's German History from 1919–1945, which maintain for me the impressions, memories and actions that remain existential for me, no matter what the changed circumstances.

In Christian teaching, which, in contrast to the decreed brainwashing at school almost opened a discourse, we debated what is respectable in view of all people (Romans 12,17). The world appeared, despite of all the misery and even under the conditions of totalitarian omnipotence, to be full of encouraging contradictions – for example in the life stories of people who had survived the War. The former

---

[6]ibid. p. 99.

officer of the imperial army, later pacifist theologian of the avowedly anti-Nazi Protestant (Bekennenden) Church, the president of the Church in Hesse during my childhood, Martin Niemöller, was, for an intensive period, such an inspiring role model for me with regard to what seems necessary above all, the ability to change. (When I later, as an adolescent, saw the pastor march, as traitor to himself, on the other side of the barricade, this was a disappointment that I was unable to foresee as a child). I understood from Niemöller's behavior and from the rumors about the assassins in the Wolfsschanze 1944, that it is a sin not to do what is good. He preached that not to do evil does not mean at all to do good. That was a good thing also for a child to be aware of, in the chaos of the time, in which to say what one thought would perhaps not straight away cost ones life, but definitely Siberia or prison for the family.

The Greek word for "preconceived" (pronoeo) can also be translated as "to notice or cogitate, or think of something in advance". Thus we could say: "be aware in advance of the good in all people". Did this not open a wide field of activity for me? I learnt, even before I knew the texts from antiquity in this context, what the "tragic" perspective is: to accept the disadvantages, suffering and losses as components of life and no to deny or mask them.

6   The more theatre texts I read, the more did I understand why a demanded behavior such as "respectable and good" – captured in the one word *kalos* – means both respectable and good.

"That you conduct your lives among the nations respectably" (1. Pet 2:12) – this demand by the Apostle seemed to me to be closely related to the diction of Grimmelshausen, Wieland, Herder, Schiller, Brecht and Kaiser. It's about the way out from the noncommitance of barbarism and civilization. Even Nietzsche, who we were forbidden to read, served, secretly, our hope. The human being is an "animal ... that may promise,"[7] he says. Its central characteristic is that it is "master of free will", yes, "sovereign", because the human being can, by way of promising, command at will about the future. According to Nietzsche, conscience of the modern human being is responsible for keeping the promise: as "dominant instinct"[8] it has the function of a moral authority.

---

[7] Friedrich Nietzsche, Zur Genealogie der Moral. In: Ders., Kritische Studienausgabe Bd. 5, Hg. V. Giorgi Colli u. Mazzino Montinari, München, 2. durchges. Aufl., 1999, p. 293.
[8] ibid. p. 294.

The political explosiveness of this explanation, for me, was that Nietzsche bind the aspect of promise to questions of law all the way to Roman law. (After I tried, without success, to sue against my occupational ban, old history, too, became a pool of counterinsurance and alienation of the present. My later productions in Greece and Cyprus, no matter whether Brecht, Borchert, Shakespeare, Euripides, Aeschylus or Sophocles, are likely to have benefited from this).

At the age of fourteen I understood, why I was summoned in from a tribunal of teachers in order to justify that I had read the forbidden *Zarathustra*. It was the power of language, the field of reference that questioned the order for those in power. I was fascinated how in *Morgenröthe* the philosopher and poet linked promising and rendering into language. For me this seemed to be, since the classical Athens, the condition for the existence of theatre. As I came to understand later, Nietzsche was concerned with the characteristics that are constitutive of promising, such as the will that triggers a promise, the language that the promise is in need of, or the conventions against which a promise is set – independent of whether the promise is to be understood as divine, as civic stipulation or as transcendental obligation. The question in itself was of enlightenment mode, and cross-grained: what kind of order is actually created through the promise: one that is legally binding, a moral one, a social, and / or one that is solely linguistic? With the help of such, as I thought, poetic dialectic and finesse the dominant disorder of promises could be led ad absurdum.

To summarize my reflections, the kernel of my experience is in particular that theatre work without a historical dimension misses its purpose. The role of cultural memory may not be of the same determining meaning at every time and at every place, but in my opinion it cannot be pushed off the stage no matter how globalized the world of theatre becomes, because the spectators will bring their own cultural memory to the performance anyway. In addition, every endeavor to conjure away the dramatic poetry from the center of contexts of experience that transcend generations, is ultimately bound to fail. This becomes evident in every case where anywhere in this world a decision has to be made about what is right and what was and is injustice. The knowledge about the unique qualities of our own heritage allies us with foreign methods and schools, which are based on their own challenges. Alienation what is respectively the other is an ancient, established correspondence of form and contents: the binding of spirit and life in the mode, in the gestus, of theatrical narration. Critique of time and society are a gift of culture, not instruments of ideological doctrine. Theatre is not the institution of enforcement for those in power, but the advocacy of the governed.

Excerpt of a video lecture, given at the plenary session, 16 May, 2009, 3rd International Conference "Consciousness, Theatre, Literature and the Arts", Lincoln University, UK, 16-18 May, 2009; Translation by Daniel Meyer-Dinkgräfe.

17 German Unity – A Settlement After 45 Years

Excerpts from an interview with Fred Lapisardi, May 2009

Lapisardi: On November 9, 1989, the Berlin Wall unexpectedly opened, less than a year later, on October 3, 1990, Germany was re-united. Both events came after decades of division that had begun with the partition of Germany into four occupation zones following its defeat in 1945 by the Four Powers—the United States, Britain, France, and the Soviet Union. Once a powerful nation, Germany lay vanquished at the end of World War II. The war's human cost had been staggering.

Haus: Millions of Germans had died or had suffered terribly during the conflict, both in combat and on the home front. Intensive Allied bombing raids, invasions, and subsequent social upheaval had forced millions of Germans from their homes. Not since the ravages of the Thirty Years' War had Germans experienced such misery. Beyond the physical destruction, Germans had been confronted with the moral devastation of defeat. In addition, the nation had to come to grips with its involvement in the Nazi atrocities.

Germans refer to the immediate aftermath of the war as the Stunde Null (Zero Hour), the point in time when Germany ceased to exist as a state and the rebuilding of the country would begin.

At first, Germany was administered by the Four Powers, each with its own oc-cupation zone. In time, Germans themselves began to play a role in the governing of these zones. Political parties were formed, and, within months of the war's end, the first elections were held. Although most people were concerned with mere physical survival, much was accomplished in rebuilding cities, fashioning a new economy, and integrating the millions of refugees, which had been forced to leave the eastern areas of Germany that had been seized by the Soviet Union and Poland after the war. The political realities of a Europe so radically rearranged presented a demanding set of challenges.

Overshadowing these events within Germany, however, was the gradual emergence of the Cold War during the second half of the 1940s. By the decade's end, the two superpowers – the United States and the Soviet Union – had faced off in an increasingly ideological confrontation.

Yes, the Iron Curtain between them cut Germany in two. Although the Allies' original plans envisioned that the territories left to Germany would remain a single state, the antagonistic concepts of political, social, and economic organization gradually led the three Western zones to join together, becoming separate from the Soviet zone and ultimately leading to the formation in 1949 of two German states. The three Western occupation zones became the Federal Republic of Germany (or West Germany), and the Soviet zone was named the German Democratic Republic (or East Germany). No doubt, we in the East felt betrayed by the West's acceptance of the division. Painfully we had to recognize, that the best way to contain Soviet expansionism was to assure the economic prosperity of the West. The success of the aid program that came to be known as the Marshall Plan deepened the rejection of the East's command economy and strengthened the trust in a free social market economy.

Can you explain in this context the role of so-called Berlin Airlift?

The Berlin Blockade (June 24, 1948 – May 11, 1949) was one of the major international crises of the Cold War. The Soviet's blocked the three Western force's railway and road access to the Western sectors of Berlin that they had been controlling. Their aim was to force the Western powers to allow the Soviet controlled regions to start supplying the Western sectors with food and fuel, thereby giving them nominal control over the entire city. In response, the Western Allies formed the Berlin Airlift to bring supplies to the inhabitants of the Western sectors. The skilled, bone wearying flying of American, British and French airmen saved the Western sectors from falling to the Soviets and helped mend German-American wounds from World War II. The success of the Airlift demonstrated that the Western forces will reject further Soviet obstruction. The Airlift was also a hope for the people in Berlin's Soviet sector and in the Soviet-controlled zone. Keep in mind, that Local elections in mid-1946 resulted in massive anti-communist protest vote. Berlin's citizens overwhelmingly elected democratic members to its city council (with an 86% majority) – strongly rejecting the election's Communist candidates. As Molotow, the Soviet foreign minister, noted, "What happens to Berlin, happens to Germany, what happens to Germany, happens to Europe". Stalin's policy of creating an Eastern block buffer zone (remember the Communist coup d'etat of 1948 in Czechoslovakia) with a weakened Germany under Soviet control culminated in autumn of 1948 in an attempted putsch for control of all of Berlin through a September 6 takeover of the city hall by SED operatives. It became impossible for the non-Communist majority in Berlin city-wide assemblies elected two years earlier to attend sessions within the Soviet sector. The elected city government was routed, with its democratic members being replaced by communist.

With their putsch the Soviet's succeeded to divide the governing of the city. In the Western sectors the democratic representatives set up a free government.

Three days after the putsch a crowd of 500,000 people gathered at the Brandenburg Gate, protesting the Soviet's and communist's actions. The airlift was working so far, but many people feared that the Allies would eventually abandon them to the Soviets. They needed reassurance that their sacrifice would not be for nothing. Mayor Ernst Reuter took the microphone and plead for his city, "You people of the world. You people of America, of England, of France, look on this city, and recognize that this city, this people must not be abandoned – cannot be abandoned!" Never before had so many Berliners gathered, the resonance worldwide was enormous. The fact that the Soviets' actions contradicted the London Conference decisions convinced the Western Allies that they must take swift and decisive measures to strengthen the parts of Germany not occupied by the Soviets. The most important result was the creation of the Federal Republic. The increasing perception among many in Europe that the Soviets posed a danger, helped to prompt the entry into NATO of most of Western Europe.

During the next four decades, the two states led separate existences. West Germany joined the Western community of nations, while East Germany became the westernmost part of the Soviet empire.

The East and West of Germany, with a common language and history, were separated by the mutual suspicion and hostility of the superpowers. In the mid-1950s, both German states rearmed. The West German armed forces, the Bundeswehr, became a vital part of the North Atlantic Treaty Organization (NATO). The East German National People's Army (Nationale Volksarmee) became a key component of the Warsaw Pact. The construction of the Berlin Wall in 1961 by the communist regime further divided the country. Barbed wire, minefields, guard towers and armed border guards illustrated the un-human nature of the status quo.

Much press time, both in print and on TV, centered around JFK's "Ich bin ein Berliner" speech. What effect did it have on the inhabitants of East Berlin?

Kennedy's speech of June 26, 1963 was a great morale boost for the West Berliners, who feared a possible Soviet occupation. Speaking from the balcony of the Rathaus Schöneberg, he said, "Two thousand years ago the proudest boast was civis Romanus sum. Today, in the world of freedom, the proudest boast is 'Ich bin ein Berliner'... All free men, wherever they may live, are citizens of Berlin, and, therefore, as a free man, I take pride in the words 'Ich bin ein Berliner!'. It is documented, that Kennedy came up with the phrase at the last moment, as well as the idea to say it in German. It is also known, that his National Security Advisor McGeorge Bundy felt the speech had gone 'a little too far' ", and the two revised the text for a softer stance before repeating the speech at the Free University later that day. The message of defiance was aimed as much at the Soviets as it was at Berliners, and was a clear statement of U.S. policy in the wake of the construction of the Berlin Wall. This was applauded by us in the East, because any rejection of Soviet imperialism boosted our inner resistance. However, Kennedy was criticized for making a speech that acknowledged Berlin's status quo as reality. The official status of Berlin at the time was that it was under joint occupation by the four Allied powers, each with primary responsibilities for a certain sector. Up to this point the U.S. had asserted that this was its status, even though the actual situation was far different. Kennedy's speech marked the first instance where the U.S. acknowledged that East Berlin was part of the Soviet bloc along with the rest of East Germany. We also were reminded, that JFK needed nearly two years to visit the city after the erection of the Wall. Decades of division had to go by until a U.S. president spoke the words East and West Berliners needed to hear. It was Ronald Reagan's demand on June 12, 1987 to Soviet leader Mikhail Gorbachev to tear down the Wall.

Both parts of Germany took a diametrical development. In West Germany, by the early 1950s a system of parliamentary democracy with free and contending political parties was firmly established. East Germany was not so fortunate. A socialist dictatorship was put in place and carefully watched by its Soviet masters.

As in the Soviet Union, political opposition was suppressed, the press censored, and the economy owned and controlled by the state. Unlike West Germany, East Germany had never free elections and was not supported by its citizens. Indeed, force was needed to keep East Germans from fleeing to the West. Between August 13, 1961 and the fall of the Wall on November 9, 1989, 186 border killings were registered. But when the Stasi archives were opened, investigators found that at least 825 people had paid with their lives for trying to escape to the West. In addition to this border killings, a number of similar political offenses were committed in the interior of East Germany: By fall 1991, 4444 cases had been registered of actual or attempted killings and about 600 000 sentences handed down by East German courts for "political offenses." Although some consolidation of the regime was assured by the construction of the Berlin Wall, the so-called "Workers and Farmers State" remained an artificial entity maintained by Soviet military power. Once this support was withdrawn, it collapsed. Remember the night of November 9, 1989: Germans from both sides climbed up the Wall. They embraced each other and sang and danced in the streets. Germans from the East immediately began pouring into the West. Within a few days, over 1 million persons per day had seized the chance to re-claim unity with their Western brothers and sisters.

These pictures went all over the world and became a symbol for the peaceful revolution of 1989. Many commentators in the West were surprised about the inner strength of the masses and their clear direction towards re-unification. After all during the four decades of division, relations between the two German states were reserved and sometimes hostile. The citizens on both sides the Wall had limited direct contact with one another. How was it possible to keep human and national relations alive? What determined the "long breath" and the ability to act in the right moment of history for ending the post-War-order?

You are right, at times, during the 1960s, for example, contact was reduced to a minimum. But even in the hardest periods, it helped, that the majority of Germans in the East stayed aware, that the division of the country and the inner order in their part was directly linked to the post-War-decisions of the Four Powers. This strong historical consciousness ensured my generation against the agitation and propaganda of the regime and its claim of an independent and alternative German nation. Western radio and TV helped to stay informed and to de-mask the communist misrule. Last but not least correspondence between families and friends across the border (for party members forbidden) were a strong link for the majority of the population. What ever happened in the East was measured against the developments in the West. One also has to remember, that aside from the restrictions against contacts between the citizens, the regime continued the special "intra-German" economic ties (Interzonenhandel) to be better off than the rest of the Soviet satellites. During the 1970s, however, the two peoples began to mix more freely as their administrations negotiated treaties that made relations between the two states more open. During the 1980s, although relations continued to improve and contacts between the two peoples became more frequent, persons attempting to flee from East Germany still died along its mined borders, the regime continued to harass and arrest dissidents, and the Socialist Unity Party of Germany (Sozialistische Einheitspartei Deutschlands – SED) rigidly controlled political life. The SED's "shield and sword", was its State Security Service (Staatssicherheitsdiens, Stasi). When the regime collapsed, the Stasi had 102 000 full-time officers and noncommissioned personal on its rolls, including 11 000 members of its special guards regiment. Between 1950 and 1989, a total of 274 000 persons served in the Stasi.

The world could not believe what kind of machinery of oppression, espionage, and international terrorism and subversion had been established over four decades. According to Simon Wiesenthal, who has been hunting Nazi criminals for half a century, "The Stasi was much, much worse than the Gestapo, if you consider only the oppression of its own people. The Gestapo had 40 000 officials watching a country of 80 million, while the Stasi employed 102 000 to control only 17 million."

The story is even worst. Let's not forget the regular Stasi informer, the inoffizielle Mitarbeiter (IM). By 1995, 174 000 had been identified as IM, or 2.5 percent of the total population between the ages of 18 and 60. Researchers were aghast when they found that about 10 000 IM, or roughly 6 percent of the total, had not yet been reached the age of 18. Since many records were destroyed, the exact number of IMs probably will never be determined; but 500 000 was cited as realistic figure. John O. Koehler says in his Book *Stasi. The Untold Story of the East German Secret Police* "Using Wiesenthal's figures for the Nazi Gestapo, there was one officer for 2 000 people. The ratio for the Stasi was one secret policeman per 166 East Germans. When the regular informers are added, these ratios become much higher: In the Stasi's case, there would have been at least one spy watching every 66 citizens!" And I do not quote here the estimates for part-time-informers, but at least one informer per 6.5 citizen is reflecting how every aspect and moment of life was under control by the State Security apparatus. If you stood the millions of files upright in one line, they would stretch for 202 kilometers. In those files you can find an unbelievable number of Stasi victims and their tormentors. The regime fulfilled completely, what Hannah Ahrendt defined as "totalitarian": it could exist only through its total government, when it opened up to democratic process in November of 1989, it fall apart like a Potemkin village after rain.

In a comment about your recent theatre text, a chorus, titled Decomposition At A Distance On The Record or Sleep's Murderer Black Sun *, you describe the regimes aim as "decomposition" of people. You summarize: "Decomposition meant blocking people from acting. It meant paralyzing them as citizens by convincing that every-thing was controlled. It meant the relentless application of a quiet coercion leading to compliance". How could one fight to become mouldable by the regime?*

My generation, born during the war and trapped in the Soviet Zone, was not only traumatized by the dreadful experience of war, but confronted with the Nazi history. For the sake of the future we became thirsty for truth and freedom. Most of us took a pacifist and antiwar stand. We had to learn to live up to our national responsibility. Our Hellenic-Christian identity and the Weimar classical heritage helped to develop an anti-totalitarian mindset. Rejecting any brain washing and manipulation was one of the basic attitudes. From its first day, May 8, 1945, the day of the German army's unconditional capitulation, until its last day, November 9, 1989, the fall of the Berlin wall, one did not need special faculties to experience and define the regime as a second German dictatorship. The Red Army and its German collaborators did all to understand this.

To live up to suppressed ideals such as freedom, justice and democracy must have been most difficult. How did you handle it with dignity as well as through compromise in your every day existence within the system?

In the beginning it was the experience of the Soviet occupation and later the regime's everyday realization in school, at work, in public life, which trained to discover the contradictions between the words and the actions of the oppressors. The permanent training of hiding your thoughts split the private from the official life. But the web of secrets and lies also resulted in character destruction. There was unbelievable waste of life time. And many got tired and gave up the hope to see the gulag disappear. We had also to recognize that Western politics do not care about suppressed people, if it is not in their interests. A growing apathy and inac-tion had been driven by a series of traumatic events. Remember. The first was the 1953 uprising, when thousands of German in the East were imprisoned and many were shot. The Soviet Army smashed the insurrection, and the Western powers limited themselves to verbal protests. In 1956, we witnessed the Soviet invasion of Hungary while the West stood idly by. The promise made by U.S. Secretary of State, John Foster Dulles, that the US would "help those who help themselves" turned out to be empty as far as the "captive nations" were concerned. The Hungarian's anguished cries for help, broadcast over Budapest radio, went unheeded. In 1961, when Germans from the East left en masse into the West, the Wall was build to stop their exodus. President John F. Kennedy, cowed by Soviet Premier Nikita S. Khrushchev at a summit in Vienna two months earlier, agonized for three days before telling the U.S. forces in Berlin to do nothing. Seven years later, the "Prague Spring" of 1968 was turned into another ice age through the Warsaw Pact invasion, including the People's Army of East Germany. But the events also confirmed, that there can't be socialism with human face. With Solidarnocz, Charta 77 and a Polish Pope in the Vatican a renewed anti-communist civic movement developed all over the Soviet empire. No doubt in the 1950s and 1960s , we often asked ourselves, why the West took so little nonmilitary measures to demonstrate its staunch opposition, instead of communicating virtual acquiescence. But it also reminded us, that an on-going division of the continent is a temporary historical circumstance, which will change, if all former Allied Forces will accept a formal end of the after-war status and the return of a unified Germany into the European family.

The efforts of Soviet president Mikhail Gorbachev, beginning in the mid-1980s, to liberalize the Soviet Union and reform its economy were met with hostility by the East German leadership. Word of these measures nevertheless reached East German grassroots opposition groups.

One example for the new level of risk taking I remember happened during an official party ritual in front of Western TV cameras on January 17, 1988, when civil rights activists opened up a banner with Rosa Luxemburg's famous words: "Freedom is always the freedom of the dissident." Plainclothed Stasi police tore down the banner and 120 demonstrators were arrested in the following melee. The party and Stasi alike reacted remorselessly to the incident. Further arrests followed and several regime critics were expelled to West Germany. Many historians consider this crackdown against independent opinion being voiced as the germ of East Germany's peaceful revolution the following year. A small group of people had mustered the courage to express their protest. From then on, that handful would grow inexorably in number. In spite of Honecker's declaration as late as January 1989 that "The Wall will stand in fifty and also in hundred years," the effects of glasnost and perestroika had begun to be evident in the Soviet Union and throughout Eastern Europe. The East German regime's frantic attempts to reject reality was obvious again in Berlin, on October 7, 1989, when it celebrated the fortieth anniversary of the foundation of its existence. In his address, Honecker sharply condemned West Germany for interfering in the East's internal affairs and for encouraging protesters, and absurdly proclaimed: "Socialism will be halted in its course neither by ox, nor ass". The prophetic retort of Gorbachev, who was present at the event, reflected imminent realities: "He who comes too late will suffer the consequences of history." By the second half of 1989, the East German opposition already consisted of a number of groups with a variety of aims and was strong enough to stage large demonstrations. The consequences of not having held in check the earlier large demonstrations against the regime's inflexibility came October 9, 1989, when 70 000 protesters shouting "We are the people" demonstrated in Leipzig. When the Soviet Army stood back and the police took no action during these historic hours, it became clear to everyone that the days of the second German dictatorship were numbered. After the crowds in Leipzig reached over 100 000 protesters on October 16, Honecker resigned and all actions against demonstrators were discontinued.

Obviously such gestures for dialogue and change (Wende) came too late. The consequences of history had opened an all-European orbit of freedom, prosperity, peace and security.

The massive flow of East Germans to the West through neighboring socialist countries in the summer and fall of 1989, particularly through Hungary, was telling evidence of a growing public opposition to the regime. In combination with crushing economic problems, and told by the Soviet leadership not to expect outside help in quelling domestic protest, the regime collapsed under massive and constantly growing public demonstrations. After elections in the spring of 1990, the opposition, the Christian-democratic "Alliance for Germany" took over the government. As a precondition for German unity, the Two-Plus-Four Talks among the two German governments and the four victorious powers of World War II began on May 5. Held in four sessions, the last which was on September 12, the talks culminated in the signing of the Treaty of the Final Settlement with Respect to Germany (the Two-Plus-Four Treaty). These talks settled questions relating to the eastern border of Germany, the strength of Germany's military forces, and the schedule of Allied troops withdrawal from German soil. In a cordial meeting between Gorbachev and Chancellor Kohl on July 16, unified Germany's membership in NATO and its full sovereignty were conceded by the Soviet president. The post-War-order came finally to an end. On October 3,

1990, the Soviet-puppet regime ceased to exist, and its territory and people were finally able to join the Federal Republic of Germany. The division of our nation that had lasted decades was ended.

Pre-published in two parts in Apofsi, Nicosia, Cyprus, October and November issues, 2009.

18 Suggested Literature

A good starting point for readers seeking to learn more about the founding, consolidation, and final reunification of the two German states is *Germany from Partition to Reunification* by Henry Ashby Turner, Jr. Another concise and expert account is Peter Pulzer's *German Politics, 1945-1995*. Longer accounts by noted historians are Volker Rolf Berghahn's *Modern Germany*, which starts with events at the turn of the century and ends in the mid-1980s, and Mary Fulbrook's *The Divided Nation*, which begins with the aftermath of World War I and ends with unification. Fulbrook's *The Two Germanies, 1945-1990* is a concise survey of the many ways historians have interpreted recent German history.

Dennis L. Bark and David R. Gress's detailed two-volume *A History of West Germany* is widely available. David Childs's *The GDR: Moscow's German Ally* is a highly readable history of the German Democratic Republic. Mary Fulbrook's *Anatomy of a Dictatorship* examines the nature of the East German state and how it failed.

A useful documentation of the postwar years and the question of reunification can be found in *The German Question*, edited by Walther Hubatsch, with Wolfgang Heidelmeyer et al. Timothy Garton Ash's *In Europe's Name* is a searching analysis of Ostpolitik, from Adenauer to Kohl. Konrad H. Jarausch provides a concise account of the events of 1989 and 1990 in his scholarly *The Rush to German Unity*. Stephen F. Szabo's *The Diplomacy of German Unification* is a good brief account of the international aspects of unification. A more detailed treatment of this subject is *Germany Unified and Europe Transformed* by Philip Zelikow and Condoleezza Rice.

Three books, which should not be overlooked by anyone interested in the peaceful revolution, are the following:
G. Jonathan Greenwald: *Berlin Witness: An American Diplomat's Chronicle of East Germany's Revolution* Pennsylvania State University Press, 1993;

Charles S. Maier: *Das Verschwinden der DDR and der Untergang des Kommunismus*, S. Fischer, 1999;

Ehrhart Neubert: *Unsere Revolution. Die Geschichte der Jahre 1989/90*, Piper, 2008.

All those who oppose intellectual truths merely stir up the fire; the cinders fly about and set fire to that which else they had not touched.

Johann Wolfgang von Goethe
1749–1832

Berlin Wall Timeline

May 8, 1945   World War II is over and Berlin is divided into 4 sectors: the America, British, and French in the West and the Soviet in the East.

June 30, 1946   At the instigation of the Soviet Military administration the demarcation line between East and West Germany is safeguarded.

October 29, 1946   A 30 day valid Interzonenpass is required to travel between the occupation zones in Germany.

June 23, 1948   Currency reform in Berlin, Berlin is divided.

June 24, 1948   Begin of the Berlin blockade.

June 25, 1948   Berlin Airlift begins.

May 12, 1949   End of Berlin blockade.

May 24, 1949   Federal Republic of Germany is founded (West Germany).

September 30, 1949   End of Berlin Airlift.

October 7, 1949   German Democratic Republic is founded (East Germany).

May 26, 1952   Border between East and West Germany and between East Germany and West Berlin is closed. Only the border between East and West Berlin is still open.

Berlin Wall Timeline

June 17, 1953   Uprising of East Berlin construction workers against the imposition of increased working norms, suppression by Red Army tanks.

November 14, 1953   The Western Powers waive the Interzonenpass, the Soviet Union follows, but East German citizen need a permission to travel to the West.

December 11, 1957   Leaving East Germany without permission is forbidden and violations are prosecuted with prison up to three years.

August 13, 1961   The Berlin sectorial border between East and West Berlin is closed, barriers are built.

August 14, 1961   Brandenburg Gate is closed by fortified fences, gun positions and watchtowers heavily guarded and patrolled. More than 200 people die in the years that followed trying to cross the wall.

June 26, 1963   President J. F. Kennedy visits Berlin and says: "Ich bin ein Berliner." ("I am a Berliner.")

December 17, 1963   West Berliner citizen may visit East Berlin the first time after more than two years.

September 3, 1971   Four Power's Agreement over Berlin, visiting becomes easier for East Berliners.

June 12, 1987   President Ronald Reagan visits Berlin and urges Soviet leader Mikhail Gorbachev to tear down the Berlin Wall.

September 10, 1989   Hungarian government opens border for East German refugees.

November 9, 1989   Berlin Wall opens. Thousands of Germans from the East stream into West Berlin. People begin to pull the Wall down in celebration.

December 22, 1989 Brandenburg Gate is opened.

October 3, 1990 Germany is formally reunited.

Heinz-Uwe Haus

Theatre director, Cultural Studies and Theatre scholar; since 1997 Professor at the Professional Theatre Training Program (PTTP) and the Theatre Department of the University of Delaware, Newark (USA).

Educated and trained in Germany at the Film Academy Potsdam- Babelsberg (Acting), as well as at the Humboldt-Universität in Berlin (Cultural Studies, German Literature and Theatre Science).

Dr. Haus began his artistic and academic career as director at the Deutsches Theater, Berlin, and founding member of the East German Directing Institute.

His productions include plays of the Ancient Greeks, Shakespeare, German classics, Brecht and the Expressionists, performed both in Germany and such countries as Canada, Cyprus, Finland, Greece, Italy, Turkey and the USA. Some of these productions have appeared in Festivals throughout Europe.

Dr. Haus has been a guest professor at more than a dozen North American universities (such as NYU, Villanova, CSUN and the University of Washington) and has given more than 500 lectures and workshops worldwide. Besides publishing in his field, he writes about intercultural and political topics in German, English and Greek medias.

His literary texts and poetry as well as his work as painter (partly under his pseudonym Jean Bodin) are only recently made known to a wider international audience.

Dr. Haus is Honorary Member of the Cyprus Centre of the International Theatre Institute and Honorary Citizen of the Greek community Katohi. In 2005 he received the Best Director Theatre Award THOC.

Dr. Haus was in 1989/90, a board member of the East German "Democratic Awakening" party (Demokratischer Aufbruch) and founder and representative of "The Praxis Group" in the US.

1992–1993 he worked as founding director of the Bildungszentrum Schloss Wendgräben of the Konrad-Adenauer-Foundation.

Dr. Haus co-founded in 1986 the International Workshop and Study Center for Ancient Greek Drama in Oiniades (Greece). From 2004 until 2007 he served as Academic Chair of the Institute for Ancient Greek Drama and Theatre in Droushia-Paphos (Cyprus).

In 2000 he has been elected into the Council of the Autorenkreis der Bundesrepublik. From 1999 until 2005 he served as Vice Chair of the (German) Wilton Park organization. In 2007 he joined the International Editorial Board of Carmina Balcanica.

He has chaired the Intercultural group of ISSEI (International Society for the Study of European Ideas) since 1994 and since 1996 has been a member of its Executive Committee.

Comments on the first edition

A new edition of AWAKENING *'89 is a timely reminder of one of the most momentous changes in ideological direction of our time. The collapse of communism in Eastern and Central Europe, the reunification of Germany, and ultimately the implosion of the Soviet Union two years later reaffirmed both the irrepressibility of the human quest for freedom and the return of the European project from the historical detour of communism.*

Heinz-Uwe Haus is a passionate, but always perceptive commentator on a historical tipping-point in which he was also an active participant. He brings to the documents and speeches collected here a deep sensibility of the social, but especially the cultural, damage inflicted by communism. As one who has admired his spirit and his realism for more than 20 years, I can attest that Haus has never fallen for the simplistic notion that the end of communist dictatorship meant the automatic flourishing of democracy and progress. Amidst the real challenges of the transition, he continues to warn against romanticising the chains of the former dictatorship. This, above all, is the enduring legacy of these reflections.

Prof. Dr. David Lovell
Head, School of Humanities and Social Sciences
University of New South Wales, Australia

This volume confronts us with the personal intellectual view on a space of time – especially in Eastern Germany – which began with the civil awakening beyond the "Iron Curtain", then led to the "Peaceful Revolution" and consequently to the total change of the political landscape in Europe.
The author was a highly committed participant in that process. It is the plain credibility of an eyewitness which makes this book worth reading.

Wolfgang Stegemann
Founder and former Chair of the civic group
"Victims of Stalinism", Fürstenberg, Germany

Comments on the first edition

An enlightening edition which gives us the crystal-clear view of an excellent writer, who has actively partipated in Europe's noblest moments in modern history. Highly recommended for students of European and German politics.

Michalis Kontos
Director, Center for Scientific Dialogue and Research, Nicosia, Cyprus

As a Romanian intellectual who always held the consciousness of an European identity, I recognized in many chapters my generation's ideas and especially our perspective about what happened in Europe before and after 1989.

I was born and lived in a communist country, in a sattelite of the Soviet Union, so I believe I understand very well what Dr. Haus concludes in the Forword of his book: "no people or nations accepted any longer to be held hostage by the Soviet's strategic interests..."

In Heinz-Uwe Haus's collection of texts, the reader can depict a person who was involved in policy-making. And we can ask the readers: who could be more appropriate to write about "Identity vs. Enlightenment", about "The Dialectics of European Identity", about "German Identity and the 1989 Revolution", "Truth (as) the first step toward reconciliation", etc. better than a theater man and educator? It is obvious that theatre comprises the ideas, the feelings, and actions of mankind.

Twenty years since the real and symbolic "fall of the Berlin Wall", the philosophical and pragmatic points of view of an intellectual who was involved in the cultural life of his country and Europe, are indispensable.

Prof. Dr. Mihaela Albu
Facultatae de Jurnalism
Universitatae Spiru Haret, Bucuresti, Romania

This is a superb collection of comments by a man of keen intellect, sharp perceptions, good judgement, and an extraordinary courage of convictions. The perspectives reflect his experience as an active participant of a movement, which not only helped to bring the Wall down but fought for the re-unification of Germany from the very beginning of the peaceful revolution.

Sigmar Schollak
Novellist, Berlin, Germany

From the cataclysmic events of his times, especially within his native Germany, Haus has extracted socio-political insights which, he realizes, have shaped him as a theater

138

person: A literary work, but particularly a drama, should evoke memories not only of the dramatist's time, but also of the viewer's. A work devoid of such evocative power is, in Haus' view, not meeting its challenge. In a great drama, sensitively staged, the times themselves appear as "extras". As Haus puts it: "A theatre work without a historical dimension misses its purpose." This perspective on the interaction of world and stage — and stage and world — is, in and of itself, worth the price of admission.

Prof. Dr. Guy Stern
Director, International Institute of the Righteous
Holocaust Memorial Center, Detroit, MI, USA

In this collection of essays, lectures and interviews, Heinz-Uwe Haus, offers a unique perspective on how the road to German unity was a product of what he calls "the double past" that began in 1933 and ended in 1989 and insists on the historical responsibility of artists, intellectuals and academics to confront injustices from the point of view of those victimized by the Stasi in the former German Democratic Republic. Haus's professional background in "theatre making", coupled with his caeseless desire to translate his personal, political, artistic experiences into a universal narrative on democratic cultural transition makes this book a must read for all those who consider critique of history and politics as gifts of culture in the struggle for 'keeping the promise'. If you wonder what the promise was/is, then plunge in this timeless yet political journey of tragedy from whereever you are in the world in this very minute.

Dr. Banu Helvacioglu
Adjunct Senior Lecturer, Political Science Department
Bilkent University, Ankara, Turkey